HIPAA Pri

Compliance – Simplified

Practical Guide for Healthcare Providers and Managers

2016 Edition
September 2016

Robert K. Brzezinski

ISBN: 1537494279
ISBN-13: 978-1537494272

"Information security is a management issue that may require technical solution." Shon Harris

"It takes 20 years to build reputation and five minutes to ruin it. If you think about that, you'll do things differently". Warren Buffet

Contents

Introduction

I thought it would be appropriate to update and revise some sections based on the fact that HIPAA is coming of age (almost 21), based on reader's feedback, and based on changes and guidance in regulatory landscape – thus a 3rd edition of the HIPAA Guide.

This book is not a typical publication providing all the background information, describing definitions, proper methodologies and tools to help create adequate policies and procedures and build risk management program. This book is the doers guide to implement the risk management program and improve the information security and compliance posture of the organization. The book and associated materials should be most helpful for small and medium size businesses, covered entities and business associates. Other organizations or individuals, including CEOs, CFOs, Board members or those directly responsible for information security risk management should find it helpful as well.

This book contains a brief overview of HIPAA laws and identifies and explains distinct risk areas, to help the risk manager/security official explain the value of investment in information security, and potential impacts of security breaches, to help build business case when creating information security/compliance budget, and to help owners/ CEOs better understand privacy, security and compliance risks.

This book provides a day-by-day, and step-by-step tasks and instructions for completing risk analysis (mapped to HIPAA Standards), for developing and implementing proper policies, procedures, forms, templates and processes and fulfilling the risk management program requirements. The book provides project management timelines and examples for establishing good risk management documentation. These tools and activities will help providers and managers clarify, organize and document office tasks, responsibilities, help reduce business risk and improve regulatory compliance.

This step-by-step guide provides walk-through the HIPAA Privacy and Security standards, risk management implementation guide, risk self-assessment, HIPAA awareness quiz, and examples of policies and procedures. The collection of these documents will help:

- Understand the business risks, why and how they can be mitigated
- Standardize business processes;
- Educate staff about best practices and provide references
- Provide necessary documentation starting points
- Accelerate risk management program implementation
- Improve organization security and regulatory compliance posture
- Prepare the organization for compliance audit

Depending on the current processes and practices in the organization, the initial investment in organizing risk management work may seem significant. However, the documentation, templates and processes should make work easier in the future, will make your business more organized and enable it to respond to patients', partner's, co-workers, auditors, certification authorities or superior's inquiries faster and more accurately.

The Risk Management process is an ongoing, continuous effort, which needs to be maintained throughout the year. It includes implementation of risk mitigation activities identified throughout the year or during the periodic risk analysis. It includes staff monitoring and training, ongoing tracking of regulatory environment, technology trends and emerging security threats. Risk management is also about updating technology, policies and procedures to improve information security and business processes.

Because the threats, vulnerabilities, technology and regulations related to privacy and information security change, I encourage you to research and read as much as possible about these topics. You may consider reading some of the materials mentioned as references to this manual, and find additional information available from various HealthIT.gov, HHS.gov, AHIMA, ISACA, HIMSS, IT specific, state or federal sources. The broader knowledge will allow you to manage risk more effectively.

Successful implementation of the Risk Management requires management and leadership skills. Individual assigned with this task should take it as an opportunity to learn and grow, practice and develop project management and collaboration skills. The results of their efforts may not be immediately visible, but again risk management does not have an end date, it is not a project, it is a continuous improvement process.

This manual was first published in July of 2012 and was updated in 2013 and in 2014 to incorporate HIPAA Omnibus modifications which become effective on March 26th 2013. The covered entities and business associates must comply with applicable requirements of the HIPAA Omnibus Final Rule as it became enforceable on September 23rd 2013.

The 2016 edition provides additional clarifications and updates for e.g. accounting of disclosures, security incidents and breach notification, direct access to lab reports (CLIA), growth in cloud computing, resources, non-covered entities (NCE) etc. I expect to incorporate further changes to this manual based on users' feedback, when additional guidelines become available and as rules or technology change.

You can use this book to create your own content and templates, or visit us at ***www.bizwit.us*** *and inquire about our SimpleVCO Virtual Compliance Office toolset to help jump start your risk analysis and risk management process, to help you organize your action steps and documentation, and to help you implement systematic information security risk management process. SimpleVCO documents / templates are referenced as examples in this guide for demonstration purposes.*

CHAPTER 1 - HIPAA LAWS OVERVIEW

HIPAA Purpose

The Health Insurance Portability and Accountability Act (HIPAA) of 1996 initiated reforms of the insurance and healthcare systems in the US. The HIPAA regulations have two major purposes:

1. The Insurance Portability section of HIPAA is about changing practices of health plans and insurers regarding portability and continuity of health coverage: limiting exclusions based on pre-existing conditions, guaranteeing policy renewal, prohibiting discrimination based on health status, helping people keep insurance when they change jobs. This section pertains to the Insurance Reform.
2. The Accountability section of HIPAA is about improving the efficiency and effectiveness of the health care system, reducing administrative costs, improving Medicare and Medicaid programs, reducing fraud and abuse, improving quality of patient care through clinical data access and information availability for decision making, protecting patients' rights, privacy and security of patient's health information. This section is called Administrative Simplification.

In every day conversations, when the term HIPAA is used, it most likely pertains to the Administrative Simplification, the Accountability section of HIPAA. This book focuses on Administrative Simplification section of HIPAA, in particular on Privacy and Security rules and their enforcement.

HIPAA Regulatory Changes

While the HIPAA regulations were introduced in 1996, the healthcare environment, healthcare needs and regulatory requirements evolved over the years. Provision of various federal regulations further increased or specified HIPAA requirements. These regulations include:

- The American Recovery and Reinvestment Act of 2009 (Recovery Act or ARRA)
- Health Information Technology for Economic and Clinical Health (HITECH) Act of 2009 including number of Health Information Technology (HIT) programs focused on Health Information Exchanges (HIE), HIT Workforce and Incentive Program for Electronic Health Records (EHR) - passed as part of ARRA
- Affordable Care Act (ACA) of 2010
- 45 CFR Parts 160 and 164 Modifications to the HIPAA Privacy, Security, Enforcement, and Breach Notification Rules Under the Health Information Technology for Economic and Clinical Health Act and the Genetic Information Nondiscrimination Act (GINA)

- 2013 HIPAA Omnibus Final Rule
- CLIA Program and HIPAA Privacy Rule; Patients' Access to Test Reports effective April 7th 2014 and enforceable by October 6th 2014.

Following federal agencies within the U.S. Department of Health and Human Services (HHS) work with HIPAA closely:

- The Office of the National Coordinator for Health Information Technology (ONC for HIT)
- **Office for Civil Rights (OCR)** - privacy, security and data breach rule enforcement agency
- Centers for Medicare and Medicaid Services (CMS)

Other federal agencies whose work often relates to HIPAA include: Drug Enforcement Administration (DEA), U.S. Department of Justice (DOJ) and the U.S. Department of Commerce, National Institute of Standards and Technology (NIST), Federal Drug Administration (FDA) and **Federal Trade Commission (FTC).** Section 5 of the FTC Act is currently the primary federal statute applicable to the privacy and security practices of businesses that collect health information but are not covered entities (NCEs), who are not covered by HIPAA.

Administrative Simplification

There are four distinct areas under the Administrative Simplification section of HIPAA regulations that affect healthcare providers (covered entities - CE) and their business associates:

1. **Transaction Standards, Code Set Standards and Identifier Standards for Employers and Providers** - are about adopting transaction standards for Electronic Data Interchange (EDI) of health care data to enable data exchanges, to automate processes, lower costs and prevent fraud. Health Plan Identifier Standard (HPID) under the National Plan Identifier Rule is under development.
2. **Privacy Rule** - is about protecting patients' rights (like access to their records) and assuring privacy of patients' data. Privacy Rule talks about privacy and security of Protected Health Information (PHI) in all formats (including electronic, paper and oral).
3. **Security Rule** - is about safeguarding Protected Health Information created, transmitted and maintained in electronic format (ePHI). Security Rule requires that the **C**onfidentiality, **I**ntegrity and **A**vailability (CIA) of information are protected.
4. **Breach Notification and Enforcement Rules** - describe security incidents/data breach notification requirements for covered entities and their business associates, describe investigations, procedures and monetary penalties for violations of the HIPAA Administrative Simplification Rules.

Transaction Standards Overview

Following transactions are subject to HIPAA Transaction Standards:

• Claims and encounter information	• Enrollment and disenrollment
• Payment and remittance advice	• Referrals and authorizations
• Claims status	• Coordination of benefits
• Eligibility	• Premium payment.

In other word healthcare providers who electronically conduct these transactions are subject to HIPAA rules compliance.

Transaction Standards are described by Accredited Standards Committee (ASC) X12 Version 5010 and National Council for Prescription Drug Programs (NCPDP) Versions D.0 and 3.0 commonly known as HIPAA 5010.

Code Sets are standards used to describe specific medical data, drugs, diagnoses and procedures to be used in transactions e.g.: the Healthcare Common Procedure Coding System HCPCS (Ancillary Services/Procedures), CPT-4 (Physicians Procedures), CDT (Dental Terminology), ICD-9 (Diagnosis and Hospital Inpatient Procedures) and ICD-10, and NDC (National Drug Codes).

Identifier Standards are the Employer Identification Number (EIN) and National Provider Identifier (NPI), which must be used by healthcare industry.

Transaction Standards Enforcement

The enforcement of the Transaction and Code Set Rule (TCS) as well as Identifier Standards is delegated to the Centers for Medicare & Medicaid Services (CMS). Currently the TCS enforcement is compliant driven. The CMS investigates complaints of non-compliance, provides technical assistance and makes decisions regarding the interpretation, implementation and enforcement of related regulations. CMS acknowledges that future enforcement efforts may have to be enhanced to include compliance audits.

In general, the compliance dates for HIPAA 5010 (Version 5010 and Version D.0.), for all covered entities, was January 1, 2012. The Centers for Medicare and Medicaid Services (CMS) Office of E-Health Standards and Services (OESS) extended its enforcement discretion period till June 30, 2012. More recently the compliance date has been changed to January 1st 2013 and enforcement discretion has been extended to March 31st 2013. The compliance and enforcement dates may remain fluid in the near future.

The Affordable Care Act of 2010 (ACA) builds on the HIPAA Act of 1996 (HIPAA) and includes additional new, expanded, or revised Administrative Simplification provisions including the adoption of operating rules and standards for each HIPAA transaction. Effective dates and compliance dates will be phased in between 2012 and 2016.

While CMS was initially responsible for enforcement of the HIPAA Privacy and Security Rule, in 2009 the Secretary of the HHS delegated the enforcement authority to the Office for Civil Rights (OCR). OCR receives and investigates complaints related to HIPAA Privacy and Security, and assesses civil monetary penalties (CMP).

State Attorney General (SAG) offices have been granted HIPAA enforcement authority as well and in some states they are very active, and Federal Trade Commission (FTC) can and does pursue HIPAA privacy and security related investigations independently from OCR.

Chapter 2 - HIPAA Privacy and Security Risks

Who needs to worry about HIPAA

HIPAA Privacy, Security, Enforcement and Breach Notification Rules apply to covered entities (CE) and their Business Associates (BA).

Covered Entities (CE) include:

- Health Care Providers - Doctors, Clinics, Hospitals, Psychologists, Dentists, Chiropractors, Nursing Homes, Pharmacies... if they transmit electronic information for transaction (listed above) subject to HIPAA Transaction Standards;
- Health Plans – Health, dental, vision insurance plans, HMO's, company and church health plans, Government programs that pay for health care, such as Medicare, Medicaid, and the military and veterans' health care programs;
- Health Care Clearinghouses - Entities that process nonstandard health information they receive from another entity into a standard (i.e., standard electronic format or data content), or vice versa.

Covered entities may disclose protected health information to other entities to help the covered entity carry out its health care functions. These individuals or entities (and their subcontractor), receiving, creating, maintaining or transmitting PHI on behalf of, or for a covered entity are called Business Associates (BA). Business Associates are obligated to appropriately safeguard the protected health information and adhere to privacy rule standards. HIPAA final rule includes Health Information Organizations (HIO), E-Prescribing Gateways, and others facilitating data transmlssion and requiring frequent access to PHI, and Vendors of Personal Health Records in business associates category.

Business Associate functions and activities include:	- claims processing or administration; - data analysis, processing, transmitting or administration; - utilization review; - quality assurance; - billing; - benefit management; - practice management; and - re-pricing

Business Associate services are:	- legal; - actuarial; - accounting; - consulting; - data aggregation; - management; - administrative; - accreditation; and - financial

Examples of Business Associates:

- Third party administrator that assists a health plan with claims processing; - CPA firm whose accounting services to a health care provider involve access to protected health information - Attorney whose legal services to a health plan involve access to protected health information - Independent medical transcriptionist that provides transcription services to a physician - HIO managing PHI exchange on behalf of CE	- Consultant that performs utilization reviews for a hospital - Health care clearinghouse that translates a claim from a non-standard format into a standard transaction on behalf of a health care provider and forwards the processed transaction to a payer - Pharmacy benefits manager that manages a health plan's pharmacist network - Data storage vendor maintaining and storing PHI, data disposal vendor

Why worry about HIPAA

Most stakeholders look at HIPAA Privacy and Security from the regulatory compliance perspective only. We look at HIPAA Privacy and Security risk management through lenses of three risk areas:

1. **Business Risks** (inability to access systems or data (ransomware), lost data and costs of data recovery (malware), cost of responding to data breach (hacking), reputation/loss of business);
2. **Patients Safety Risks** (harmful drug interactions, death, liability arising from lost or corrupted data leading to misdiagnosis);
3. **Regulatory Compliance Risks** (data collection and legal cost of responding to complaints or investigations, civil monetary penalties, criminal offense liabilities, public relations and reputation costs ("OCR Wall of Shame")).

Each of these perspectives appeals to various stakeholders more than others. Looking at all of the risk areas comprehensively helps understand that ignoring HIPAA Privacy and Security rules may create significant risk for any business, and that managing these risks is not only necessary, but also prudent.

There are number of general or "environmental" factors that help understand increased privacy and security risks, and why Covered Entities and Business Associates should worry about HIPAA regulations.

"Environmental" factors:

- Constantly increasing volume of digital assets (e.g. medical, financial records or other personally identifiable information (PII)) and increased reliance on electronic transactions;
- Increasing monetary attractiveness of ePHI ($50+ per ePHI versus $1 per credit card number or SSN). Medical identity theft or Medicare/ Medicaid fraud is more difficult to detect, illegal activities last longer and are more lucrative. Organized crime uses stolen ePHI for fraudulent tax returns, insurance fraud, illegal drug purchases and manufacturing, identity fraud;
- Increased monetary attractiveness (return on investment) of certain forms of attacks like ransomware – unfortunately people pay;
- Increased threats affecting digital assets - hacker attacks leading to data and intellectual property theft, extortion or ransom demands (ransomware), employee malicious actions resulting in harming employer by e.g. disabling network services, accidental data loss or leakage, inappropriate use of ePHI, identity and credit card theft;
- Increased mobility of ePHI - laptop and smart phone use;
- Increased complexity and cost of systems and infrastructure;
- Increased competition in healthcare industry and pressure for lowering costs.

Business Risks

The intent of HIPAA regulations is to promote good privacy and security business practices, prevent data breaches and protect businesses from unnecessary and unexpected business loses. While for some the business aspects of HIPAA regulations may not be immediately visible, the following should be considered to better understand potential Business Risks related to HIPAA non-compliance:

- Cost of data breaches (e.g. device or data theft, improper disclosure or access, hacking incident) - time spent on assessing the data breach, investigation and data forensics, legal advisory and defense costs, notification and identity protection costs, communication, public relations/reputation repair costs, increased insurance cost and data breach remediation costs;

- Inability to access systems, lost data and costs of data recovery (e.g. equipment failure, theft, malware/ ransomware) – forensics costs, lost productivity/lost business due to data or systems unavailability, ransom attacks may be a reportable data breaches;
- Reputation/loss of business - loss of business due to data breach, posting on OCR website, lost reputation, poor patient rating, lost referrals. Consider week long Hollywood Presbyterian Medical Center outage due to ransomware attack, or Target breach: sales and market value drop, and CEO/CIO resignations. High risk entities may not be allowed to participate in Accountable Care Organization (ACO) built around large healthcare system.

Examples – not to "cry wolf" just to demonstrate:

2016 California Data Breach Report indicates that most small businesses will on average lose almost 10,000 records. Based on 2015 Verizon Data Breach Investigation Report – this type of data breach will cost small company somewhere between 143K to 223K (upper level cost prediction reach over $3 M). Ponemon Institute reports indicate cost per compromised, lost record in range of $200.

2011 Massachusetts eHealth Collaborative data breach affecting almost 1,000 individuals cost $288,000 to resolve.

Costs of identity protection/credit monitoring could be around $100-$150 per year, per individual. The identity monitoring services for 5,000 individuals could cost $500,000 per year.

Class action lawsuits are $1,000 per lost record e.g. Tricare class action lawsuit is for $4.9 billion, Stanford class action litigation is for $20 million. In 2014, the Stanford Hospital & Clinics and two business associates settled for $4 million; AvMed (health plan that lost laptop in 2009) settled class action lawsuit for $3 million. The legal costs of responding to class-action are significant.

In 2016 nearly 31,000 of St. Joseph Health patients whose data was compromised in 2012 data breach **will receive class-action settlement** worth 7.5 million ($242 per individual). Total breach related expenses including attorney fees, credit monitoring, and set aside for plaintiffs were 22.5 million - plus 17 million for security upgrades.

OCR investigates and fines small providers: HONI Hospice in Idaho fined $50,000; Phoenix Cardiac Surgery fined $100,000.

State Attorney General Offices action.

In 2012 Accretive Health was fined $2.5 million for security and privacy violations, and is banned from doing business in Minnesota for two years, which translates into a loss of 46-50 million in revenues.

Massachusetts Attorney General settles improper paper record disposal HIPAA case with four pathology groups and (defunct) medical billing company for $140,000.

FTC actions - (2013) Cord Blood Bank Settles FTC Charges that it Failed to Protect Consumers Sensitive Personal Information of nearly 300K consumers; (2013) Accretive Health Settles FTC Charges That It Failed to Adequately Protect Consumers' Personal Information; (2014) Provider of Medical Transcript Services Settles FTC Charges That It Failed to Adequately Protect Consumers' Personal Information Settlement with GMR Transcription Marks the 50th Data Security Case Settled by the Agency

OCR 2016 (August) settlements reach 9 cases and 20.2 million, including first settlement with business associate Catholic Health Services (lost, non-encrypted iPhone) - 650K; North Memorial Health Care of Minnesota 1.55 M (case related to Accretive Health); and largest (to date) settlement with Advocate Health Care for 5.5 M.

"CEO Pleads Guilty in Hacking Case ... pleaded guilty to conspiring to hack into the computer systems of two competitors to improve his company's software development and sales strategy..."

"Compromise of Systems Impacted Company for a Month ... EnerVest was unable to fully communicate or conduct business operations for approximately 30 days as a result of Mitchell's acts. In addition to his four-year prison sentence, Mitchell was ordered to pay $428,000 ...

Estimated Data Breach Cost – Simple Example.
Can your business afford these costs?

Number of individual patient records maintained by organization		10,000
Legal, forensics, media and public relations costs associated with data breach – number of hours @ $150 per hour	500	$75,000
Internal research and investigation labor cost 100 hours @ $75 per hour	100	$7,500
Credit monitoring for 1 year @ $10 per individual, per month for 50% of affected individuals	$10	$600,000
Notification cost @ $1.00 per letter	$1	$10,000
TOTAL COST **WITHOUT** LITIGATION		**$692,500**
Class action litigations are $1,000 per record. The legal costs would also significantly increase.		$10,000,000
Total cost **WITH** litigation settled at 10%	10.00%	**$1,692,500**

Patient Safety

Availability of patient's data in electronic format creates opportunities for quicker and better diagnosis, lower service costs and better outcomes of medical care. These opportunities are based on the premise that the patient's safety is maintained through data security and confidentiality, when the health data is created, modified, transmitted or used:

- Patients trust that doctors will not harm them. Patients trust that technology the doctors' use will keep their personal/health information secure and confidential, thus eliminating chances for misdiagnosis, mistreatment or identity theft resulting in stress and potential financial loses.
- Trust in security of medical devices which are becoming technologically advanced and are widely used to record patients' data or administer medication. These devices, not necessarily just PCs are becoming targets for data theft. Assuring security of these devices and data is paramount to patients' safety.
- Data availability through the health information exchanges (HIE) creates tremendous opportunities. However, the data may only be available through HIE when patients' trust that the HIEs will keep their data secure and confidential. The benefits of health information exchanges can only be realized when doctors' trust the quality of the available data, so they can assure patient's safety.
- Doctors refer patients to hospitals. Will they still refer patients to hospitals that experienced data breaches or were "out of business" for extended period of time due to security incidents (ransomware)?

Regulatory Compliance

We look at regulatory compliance as a tertiary not primary risk area for HIPAA Privacy and Security. However, the importance of the regulatory compliance aspects of HIPAA should not be minimized as:

- Health Information Technology (HIT) is a top Federal priority and the HIPAA Rules are important in HIT successful implementation. The Federal government has strongly emphasized this in Federal Health IT strategic plans for 2011/2015 and 2015/2020 citing goals like "Inspiring Confidence and Trust in Health IT", "Expanding Adoption of Health IT and Advancing Secure and Interoperable Health Information", which really emphasize the importance of TRUST in the federal HIT investment, and Health Information Exchanges (HIE).
- HIPAA compliance is very much related to CMS Electronic Health Records incentives program (Stage 1 and Stage 2 - Meaningful Use

incentives). Attestation to completion of Security Risk Analysis is one of the 15 core criteria to qualify for the incentives.

- Accountable Care Organizations (ACO) concept largely depends on successful exchange of information through HIE. Allowing risky participants not meeting HIPAA compliance, to participate in ACO would be an unnecessary and easily avoidable risk. A documented risk management plan and some form of attestation to overall HIPAA compliance may be required before being accepted into ACO.
- HIPAA is the law. It is a Legal regulatory requirement that carries civil and criminal penalties. These penalties can be as high as 1.5 million per identical incidents during one year. The criminal penalties enforced by Department of Justice range from 1 to 10 years in prison.

Privacy and security gaps, lack of training, policies and procedures, and privacy and security awareness, lack of basic risk management steps can result in significant civil monetary penalties impacting the business side of the organization.

Multiple federal regulations and agencies focused on protection of individually identifiable information in the last few years. The Red Flags Rule requires many businesses (e.g. insurance companies) to implement Identity Theft prevention program designed to identify "red flags" of identity theft in day-to-day operations. Federal Trade Commission (FTC) leads the enforcement of these rules and offers many fraud and identity theft prevention resources.

HIPAA Enforcement

The Department of Health and Human Services' (HHS) Office for Civil Rights (OCR) is responsible for the enforcement of the HIPAA Privacy, Security, Enforcement and Breach notification rules since 2009.

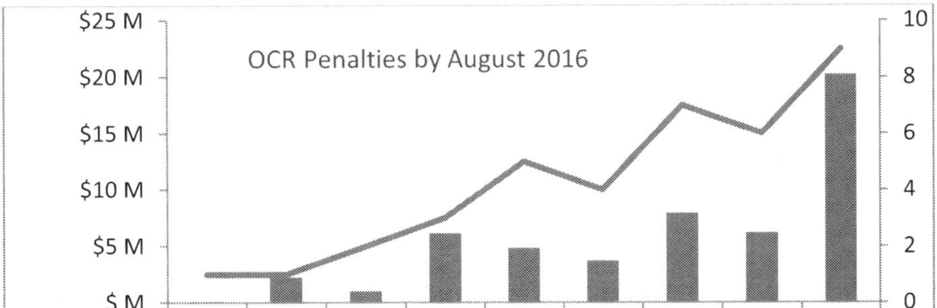

	2008	2009	2010	2011	2012	2013	2014	2015	2016
Amount	.1 M	2.3 M	1.0 M	6.2 M	4.9 M	3.7 M	7.9 M	6.2 M	20.2 M
Resolutions	1	1	2	3	5	4	7	6	9

The OCR HIPAA enforcement is described on OCR page (see link below), the chart above is based on the **Resolution Agreements** data. **Case**

Examples are good review of issues found during OCR investigations triggered by data breach reports or complaints. Review Enforcement Data, specifically **Top 5 Issues in Investigated Cases**. Partial data shown below points out to growing need for Focus On Security as Issue 5 relates to increased number of cyber security attacks on healthcare.

Year	Issue 1	Issue 2	Issue 3	Issue 4	Issue 5
2014	Impermissible Uses & Disclosures	Safeguards	Administrative Safeguards	Access	Technical Safeguards
2013	Impermissible Uses & Disclosures	Safeguards	Access	Administrative Safeguards	Minimum Necessary
2012	Impermissible Uses & Disclosures	Safeguards	Administrative Safeguards	Access	Minimum Necessary

http://www.hhs.gov/hipaa/for-professionals/compliance-enforcement/index.html

The OCR Data Breach Portal allows organizations and individuals to file a data breach report and to see information about data breach reports affecting more than 500 individuals, and reported to OCR – sometimes referred to as "Wall of Shame".

https://ocrportal.hhs.gov/ocr/breach/breach_report.jsf

As of August 2016 there were 1,639 incidents reported on the Wall of Shame, more than 53% of them resulting from loss or theft of device containing PHI, and some resulting from loss/theft of paper/film media.

Count of Reported Data Breaches

Type of Breach	Total	%
Hacking/IT Incident	214	13.1%
Improper Disposal	60	3.7%
Loss or Theft	878	53.6%
Unauthorized Access/Disclosure	372	22.7%
Other / Unknown	115	7.0%
Grand Total	**1639**	**100.0%**

These incidents affected over 166.5 million records, and as you see below, most records were compromised due to Hacking / IT Incidents. 2015 data breaches of large insurance companies like Anthem (79M), Excellus (10M) and Premera (11M) contributed to this statistic.

Sum of Individuals Affected

Type of Breach	Total	%
Hacking/IT Incident	125,077,637	75.1%
Improper Disposal	953,980	0.6%
Loss or Theft	31,544,250	18.9%
Unauthorized Access/Disclosure	5,620,377	3.4%
Other / Unknown	3,376,810	2.0%
Grand Total	**166,573,054**	**100.0%**

OCR Audits http://www.hhs.gov/hipaa/for-professionals/compliance-enforcement/audit/index.html

OCR website provides info on 115 Phase 1 audits completed in 2012. In July 2016 **OCR started Phase 2** of the audit program, which ultimately may become a permanent HIPAA Privacy, Security and Compliance audit program. Selected covered entities received notifications of being selected for an audit and were asked to provide (upload) necessary information into OCR portal. They were also asked to provide listing of their business associates as OCR plans to commence **business associates audits** in the fall of 2016.

The focus of the desk audits (offsite) is on:

Requirements Selected for Desk Audit Review	
Privacy Rule	Notice of Privacy Practices & Content Requirements
	Provision of Notice – Electronic Notice
	Right to Access
Breach Notification Rule	Timeliness of Notification
	Content of Notification
Security Rule	Security Management Process - Risk Analysis
	Security Management Process - Risk Management

For details Select Protocol Elements on OCR website. Covered entities were given 10 business days to provide requested info, and were asked to respond accurately, to the point rather than submitting volumes of documentation.

I expect that during business associates audit, OCR will ask for similar information, and that the notice of privacy practice/provision of notice, will be replaced with ask for business associate agreements with covered entities and with sub-contractors.

The final HIPAA rule makes business associates (and their subcontractors) explicitly liable for HIPAA compliance and civil monetary penalties. Covered entities and business associates must comply with HIPAA final rule after September 23rd 2013. During our risk analysis and consulting engagements we are still finding lots of business associates non-compliance issues and I'm sure OCR investigations identify similar issues.

For organizations, which have the documentation organized, that have the risk management process in place, responding to audit request will not be difficult. Top 5 Issues investigated in OCR cases will most likely drive the direction of OCR audit program. The 2014 OCR HITECH Act Report to Congress points out to major deficiencies in following areas - another audits direction driver:

Privacy: Notice of Privacy Practices Access of individuals Minimum Necessary Authorizations	Security: Risk Analysis Media Movement and Disposal Audit Controls and Monitoring

http://www.hhs.gov/ocr/privacy/hipaa/enforcement/compliancereport2011-2012.pdf

The OCR enforcement efforts also include complaint investigations and assessments of civil monetary penalties, and enforcement training completion for State Attorneys General staff to broaden rule enforcement capabilities.

The Office of Inspector General (OIG) in 2012 conducted review of the CMS Meaningful Use HIT incentives payments for EHR program. The OIG identified weaknesses in program monitoring, which resulted in increased CMS auditing activities of the incentives payment program.

Federal Trade Commission (FTC) is often involved in data/identity theft cases, they are responsible for implementation of Section 5 of the Federal Trade Commission Act - Commission enforces the proscription against unfair or deceptive acts or practices. FTC can pursue investigations independently from HHS/OCR.

FTC "standard" resolution is long term independent auditing/ monitoring requirement. In CVS, Rite Aid and Accretive Health cases the monitoring and reporting requirement were extended to 20 years. Companies have to conduct independent audits every other year and report to FTC – this is significant operational and reporting burden and cost for companies affected.

It is important to understand and communicate to staff potential penalties resulting from non-compliance, and impact of these penalties on the organization e.g. potential workforce reductions and/or business hardship /bankruptcy.

TABLE 1—CATEGORIES OF VIOLATIONS AND RESPECTIVE PENALTY AMOUNTS AVAILABLE		
Violation category—Section 1176(a)(1)	Each violation	All such violations of an identical provision in a calendar year
(A) Did Not Know	$100-$50,000	$1,500,000
(B) Reasonable Cause	$1,000-$50,000	$1,500,000
(C)(i) Willful Neglect—Corrected	$10,000-$50,000	$1,500,000
(C)(ii) Willful Neglect—Not Corrected	$50,000	$1,500,000

In addition to civil monetary penalties assessed by OCR or State Attorney General, the Department of Justice (DOJ) can also enforce criminal penalties for certain actions. The DOJ criminal penalties include monetary penalty and also prison sentences.

Summary of DOJ penalties

Offense	Monetary penalty	Prison term
For certain offenses such as knowingly obtaining PHI	Up to $50,000 and	Up to 1 year
If the offenses are committed under false pretenses	Up to $100,000 and	Up to 5 years
If the offenses are committed with the intent to sell, transfer, or use protected health information for commercial advantage, personal gain, or malicious harm	Up to $250,000 and	Up to 10 years

It is a good practice to use the above information in associates training along with real live examples of DOJ penalties enforcement e.g. case of two individuals sentenced to 26 and 10 years in prison for stealing PII from South Miami Hospital and filing over 2,000 false tax returns seeking over $11 million in refunds.

! Almost all of the violations listed below, cited lack of adequate policies and procedures (including sanction policy), and lack of employee training as major shortcomings of HIPAA compliance. In addition to CMPs the entities had to create and report the implementation of the Corrective Action Plans (CAP). They are also usually subject to 3 year monitoring and reporting plan. All HHS/OCR settlement agreements and cases are available at:

http://www.hhs.gov/hipaa/for-professionals/compliance-enforcement/agreements/index.html

The following are few examples of settlement agreements and civil monetary penalties (CMP) assessed by OCR against various entities:

Year	Entity	Penalty	Violation
2009	CVS Pharmacy Inc	2,250,000	Improper disposal of labels and prescriptions.
2011	Cignet Health of Prince George's County, MD (Cignet)	4,300,000	Denying access to medical records for 41 patients ($1 M) + lack of cooperation with OCR ($3.3 M).
2011	University of California at Los Angeles (UCLAHS)	865,500	Unauthorized employee access, snooping.
2012	Blue Cross Blue Shield of Tennessee (BCBST)	1,500,000	Loss of unencrypted backup media.
2012	Phoenix Cardiac Surgery (small)	100,000	Lack of HIPAA safeguards, policies and procedures.
2012	Alaska DHHS	1,700,000	Lack of risk analysis, encryption, training and other policies and procedures
2013	HONI Hospice of North Idaho	50,000	Loss of unencrypted laptop, less than 500 individuals affected
2013	Affinity Health Plan, Inc.	1,215,780	Did not delete data/sanitize copiers before returning them to lessor
2013	Adult & Pediatric Dermatology, P.C	150,000	Loss of unencrypted thumb drive, policy and training deficiencies
2014	County Government Skagit County, Washington	215,000	Unauthorized access to ePHI on public server, failure to provide breach notification
2014	Concentra Health Services	1,725,220	Unencrypted laptop stolen
2014	New York Presbyterian (NYP)	3,300,000	ePHI accessible to internet search engines
2014	QCA Health Plan, Inc., of Arkansas	250,000	Stolen unencrypted laptop
2014	Columbia University Medical Center	1,500,000	Failure to conduct risk analysis and implement process for assessing and monitoring IT systems.
2016	Catholic Health Care Services (BA)	650,000	Unencrypted iPhone stolen
2016	Advocate Healthcare	5,500,000	Stolen devices, no BAA, multiple incidents

Chapter 3 - HIPAA Privacy and Security Standards Overview

Risk Management Program

The HIPAA Privacy and Security Risk Management program is an ongoing effort of identifying and evaluating criticality of your assets, their vulnerabilities and threats these assets are exposed to. The risk management is not a one-time effort because assets and the environment constantly change, thus a continuous monitoring and assessment are necessary.

To be successful the HIPAA Privacy and Security Risk Management program needs the following:

- Top (CEO, CFO, Board) driven management support, including regular information privacy, security and compliance risk status reporting
- Dedicated individual(s) responsible for implementation of risk management program
- Clear communication strategy to make entire organization responsible for risk management

The Risk Management program is a continuous effort, which can be divided in following cycles:

- Risk Analysis – which allows for assets, threats and vulnerabilities identification and periodic evaluation. Risk analysis identifies security gaps, compliance issues and creates a Risk Profile for the organization. Based on the entity Risk Profile and cost benefit analysis the Risk Mitigation Plan is developed. The Risk Mitigation Plan recommends actions (mitigation, acceptance or deferral) for addressing specific risks. Periodic internal or 3rd party Risk Analysis allows for evaluation of the Risk Management Program effectiveness.
- Risk Management Program (Plan) - is not only a project management plan for implementation of the Risk Mitigation Strategies identified in the Risk Mitigation Plan. It is also an ongoing set of risk management activities. These activities address how the organization deals with specific risks and documents how it meets regulatory compliance standards.
- Updating policies, standards, guidelines and procedures - is necessary to align documentation and risk mitigation activities with frequently changing regulations, standards and environment e.g. use of cloud services. These efforts will be part of the Risk Management Program, but because of their significance they need to be emphasized.

- Employee training and reminders - are necessary to communicate staff responsibilities and provide reference for best practices. The trainings and reminders are some the most effective ways to improve the risk posture of the organization, and are the most often cited requirements for improvement of risk management programs in OCR resolution agreements.

The **executive leadership** of the organization may initially "invest" very little in risk management program. The initial investment may be limited to identifying the individual (risk manager/security official) responsible for meeting the compliance requirements. It will be the risk manager task to explain different risk areas (business risk, patient safety and regulatory compliance) and their potential impacts on the organization. This approach supported with cost-benefit analysis for recommended risk mitigation strategies could be effective in securing necessary resources to improve security posture and minimize risk exposure for the organization.

In the following sections we will look at HIPAA Privacy and Security Risk Management from the perspective of the administrative, physical, technical safeguards and organizational requirements, and we'll go through implementation specifications for each specific standard. We will mention approaches and/or documentation, which is required or which would be helpful in meeting compliance requirements. Having appropriate documentation updated and readily available will:

- Make responding to OCR, FTC or State Attorney General (SAG) audit/request for information easier, timely and less stressful;
- Improve service by responding to patients' inquiries/requests faster;
- Improve asset inventory/tracking, inventory management;
- Meet regulatory requirements;
- Make your company more efficient by having replicable, documented standards and processes for reference, training and organizational improvement;
- Improve staff awareness about privacy, information security, promote ethical behaviors and minimize associated risks.

The above accomplishments will help you earn "gold stars" with your key stakeholders e.g. C-level leadership, Board of Directors. Risk management will not happen, if you as an owner or CEO, are not going to take certain level of risk management ownership, keep designated staff accountable and follow up on it.

Risk Management starts with Risk Analysis

HIPAA Security Rule is described in §164.306 - §164.316

HIPAA Breach Notification Rule is described in §164.402 - §164.414.

Before fully engaging in Risk Management it is prudent to identify in writing the Security Official who will be responsible for HIPAA Security Rule compliance in the organization. This step will allow the organization to meet the §164.308(a)(2) Assigned Security Responsibility standard. Depending on the size of the organization the privacy and security risk management responsibilities may be assigned to Chief Privacy (Ethics) Officer and Chief Information Security Officer, Chief Security Officer or Chief Information Officer. In smaller organizations the Privacy/Security Official roles may be shared by office manager or practice owner, but it is important to document this responsibility.

Risk Management starts with an accurate assessment of the organization risks - Risk Analysis.

Risk analysis and risk assessment terms are often used interchangeably. However, to provide more clarity, the OCR tends to use the risk assessment term in context of data breaches, when completion of risk assessment is required to determine the probability of PHI compromise. We'll take similar approach and use the term risk assessment in context of data breaches, and use the risk analysis term as a snapshot of your risk management efforts.

§164.308(a)(1) Security Management Process is one of the required HIPAA Security Rule standards.

- Risk Analysis §164.308(a)(1)(ii)(a) is one of the implementation specifications for this standard listed under the Administrative Safeguards, and it requires that entities conduct an accurate and thorough assessment of the potential risks and vulnerabilities to the confidentiality, integrity, and availability of electronic protected health information held by the covered entity.

Conducting a comprehensive Risk Analysis and focusing on security practices rather than just technology, will provide a strategic perspective, will make risk management more effective and can make it more efficient.

The individual responsible for the risk management will have to decide whether the risk analysis will be conducted with internal resources or through the third party. When selecting a vendor, it might be a good idea to select one who can also assess organization HIPAA Privacy Rule compliance. The benefit of the periodic third party assessment is the objective, unbiased perspective. Independent third party assessments are frequently part of the resolution agreements with OCR. When self-assessment tools are used it might be beneficial to have a third party complete a periodic review of the organization self-assessment.

The company size, resources and data availability will drive the selection of risk analysis tools and methodologies. There are two distinct risk analysis methodologies:

- Quantitative risk analysis is based on assigning dollar values to assets, estimating potential loss per threat (single loss expectancy SLE), estimating annual rate of occurrence (ARO) and calculating annual loss potential per threat (annual loss expectancy ALE). While the quantitative risk analysis approach can be very "precise" and provides dollar values for cost/benefit discussions, it can be extremely laborious with complex calculations and values not easily understood. This approach incorporates assumptions, estimates and probabilities.
- Qualitative risk analysis walks through different risk scenarios, looks at assets criticality and threat agents, ranks the threats, vulnerabilities and their potential impact. The subject matter experts collect information and develop the risk profile using checklists, questionnaires and interviews. The Operationally Critical Threat, Asset, and Vulnerability Evaluation (OCTAVE) methodology developed by CERT at Carnegie Mellon University is an example of qualitative risk-based strategic assessment and planning tool for security. Supplementing the qualitative risk analysis with cost/benefit calculations for recommended mitigation strategies, simple risk impact estimates and/or industry examples e.g. settlement agreements, incident cases can effectively and efficiently address the need for quantifying security risks.

While a detail walk through various risk analysis methodologies is out of the scope of this book, the implementation steps for risk analysis will be discussed later. The following are common activities during risk analysis process:

- Identifying and ranking risk measurement criteria and impact values (high, medium, low) for the following impact areas: reputation/ customer confidence, financial, productivity, safety/health, fines/legal penalties, in other word estimating risk appetite;
- Identifying and ranking critical information assets (hardware, software, systems, networks, sensitive data; identifying systems' vulnerabilities (missing updates/ security features, misconfiguration); documenting hardware/ software inventory;
- Documenting workforce (e.g. training completion, contact info, system access);
- Identifying threats, threat agents and/or threat scenarios, identifying frequency of threats;
- Reviewing business processes, access management and system activity review processes, system's capabilities or awareness and availability of policies and procedures (completing questionnaires);

- Completing walk-through audits assessing physical security and security compliance;
- Identifying risks, completing risk profile and identifying risk mitigation strategies.

Documentation of Risk Analysis process and its completion will be required during audit. The risk mitigation strategies identified in the Risk Analysis will help develop the Risk Management Program and implement various risk management measures/activities discussed below in context of HIPAA rules and standards.

Privacy Rule compliance

The comprehensive risk analysis should evaluate the HIPAA Privacy Rule compliance, and before addressing security risks identified in risk assessment or other HIPAA Security Rule standards, it is good to spend some time on the HIPAA Privacy Rule described in §164.502 - §164.530. Organizations should formally identify an individual responsible for Privacy Rule enforcement. Smaller organizations may choose to assign the privacy and security responsibilities to one individual.

By now most organizations have revised their Notice of Privacy Practices (NPP), but some still miss required NPP elements. We suggest that you use OCR Model Notices of Privacy Practices and that you post it on your website as well, as this is one of the requirements. Business environment, privacy rule changes and clarifications necessitate that organizations review their Notice of Privacy Practices and forms supporting patients' rights.

http://www.hhs.gov/hipaa/for-professionals/privacy/guidance/model-notices-privacy-practices/index.html

Because Privacy Rule is the most customer facing regulatory requirement, it is necessary to look at it first and make sure the organization fully meets these requirements, and assure the staff is trained and aware of patients' rights, to be able to provide friendly customer service when patient's attempt to exercise their rights.

Review the content of Notice of Privacy Practices (NPP) to make sure it includes the following elements:

- Identifies and explains patients' rights to:
    - Request and receive NPP
    - Request and obtain copy of personal health records (applies to CLIA certified and exempt labs, to provide direct access to lab reports for patients)
    - Amend health information

- Authorize disclosure of health information for certain purposes including marketing
- Request a report accounting for disclosure of individual's health information
- Request to be contacted at different address or in different form
- Be notified about data breaches affecting their PHI
- Request restrictions on certain use or disclosure of PHI including restriction on disclosing PHI with health plan when services are paid out of pocket in full.
- Ask for additional information or file complaints
- Provides information how patients can exercise their rights
- Provides reasons and examples of how the organization can use or disclose health information without patient consent
- Provides information about changes to the NPP
- Provides contact information for patients for additional information requests or complaints
- Provides NPP effective date and last revision date

The NPP should be posted and available to patients' in the organization and on the company website. Supporting patients' rights requires forms and processes to be available to properly document patient's requests and organization responses to these requests. These processes should be captured in written procedures. Organization policies and procedures should also identify designated record set and legal health record elements, address minimum necessary disclosure, individuals' authentication and guidance on responding to legal/law enforcement requests for protected health information (PHI).

Organizations participating in Health Information Exchanges (HIE) should also ensure obtaining patient consent for exchanging data and assure patients access to complete health record. There are two major topics to consider in context of HIE:

- Granular consent allowing patients to agree to share specific portion of their health record;
- Consent model – opt in versus opt out. The "opt out" patient consent model allows the organization to automatically exchange all data unless patient chooses to opt out.

All company employees, but especially front desk staff interacting with patients the most, should know where the updated policies, procedures and forms are, should be trained about privacy practices, patients' rights and how to help customers exercise their rights and complete specific forms. The friendly, helpful approach can often alleviate patients' frustration and prevent complaints leading to regulatory investigations. All of the above items should cover major aspects of the HIPAA Privacy Rule requirements.

HIPAA final rule clarifies business associates (BA) responsibility to comply with Privacy rule. In general business associates do not have to identify privacy official and do not have to provide notice of privacy practices, but they have to comply with other elements of Privacy laws.

Administrative Safeguards

In the following sections we'll focus entirely on HIPAA Security and Breach Notification Rules, related standards and implementation specifications. These sections cover the administrative, physical, technical safeguards and organizational requirements.

Security Management

To fully meet the Security Management Process standard identified in HIPAA Security Rule, following key activities (implementation specifications) need to be completed:

- Risk Analysis §164.308(a)(1)(ii)(A) (Required) - discussed above;
- Risk Management §164.308(a)(1)(ii)(B) (Required) - is about implementing security measures sufficient to reduce risks and vulnerabilities to a reasonable and appropriate level. NIST Cybersecurity framework (**Identify, Protect, Detect, Respond, Recover**) can be used to develop and implement a comprehensive Risk Management Program, and communicate it to leadership. Keeping track of system's inventories, monitoring vulnerabilities, staff, contractors and partners access, updating security configuration and business associates agreements, building security awareness, constantly adapting to threats and regulatory changes ... and documenting these activities will build good foundation for risk management.
- Sanction policy §164.308(a)(1)(ii)(C) (Required) - is about developing and applying appropriate sanctions against workforce members who fail to comply with the security policies and procedures of the covered entity. Sanction policy is a standardized, documented methodology of reviewing and assessing employee non-compliance and determining sanction severity. The consistently applied and properly communicated sanction policy helps with:
    - Consistent application of disciplinary actions
    - Improves employee compliance
    - Builds public trust

  - Strengthens company position in dispute resolution
  - Strengthens company position in case of civil actions, litigations or regulatory enforcement

- Information system activity review §164.308(a)(1)(ii)(D) (Required) - is about implementing procedures to regularly review records of information system activity, such as audit logs, access reports, and security incident tracking reports. The purpose of system activity review is to identify policy violations as well as potential data breaches, and take proactive corrective actions. The following will help meet the requirement of this standard:
  - **Identify**ing reports or audit logs to review system activities e.g. new hardware/software connected to network, firewall or end point security logs, PHI system or records access logs, prescription approval reports, walk through audits.
  - Automating scanning and periodic vulnerability testing and/or implementing penetration testing (for larger organizations).
  - **Automating** log collection, correlation and review to **Detect** Indicators of Attack (IoA) and Indicators of Compromise (IoC). Security Incident and Event Management (SIEM) tools are a good way to automate the process even for small companies.
  - Developing and implementing monitoring schedule and documentation requirements including log/ reports retention.
  - Implementing monitoring reports and reporting frequency. Quarterly monitoring report presented and discussed with senior leadership formalizes and forces the documented review of the privacy and security related issues and problems in the organization. This report adds the accountability component, verifying the monitoring schedule implementation and follow up on issues. This report should be signed off and retained for HIPAA documentation purposes.
  - Continuous **monitoring** and monitoring documentation plays important role in **detecting** issues and is essential in documenting due diligence and responding to audits or investigations.

- The Assigned Security Responsibility standard §164.308(a)(2) (Required) - requires identification of the security official who is responsible for the development and implementation of the policies and procedures required by the HIPAA Security Rule. Identifying job responsibilities in position description or completion of the document identifying specific individual and her/his responsibilities, and obtaining individual's acceptance/signature will meet the standard requirements.

Specific responsibilities of the Security Official may include:

- Ensuring (privacy and) security policies, procedures, and standards are in place and adhered to by entity.
- Providing basic (privacy and) security support for all systems and users.
- Providing on-going employee (privacy and) security education.
- Performing periodic audits/log review.
- Managing system(s) users and overseeing information use.
- Reporting regularly to the Covered Entity leadership on entity's status with regard to HIPAA Privacy and Security compliance.

Security Official responsibilities are sometimes merged with Privacy responsibilities – this approach is even used in some large organization. Chief Information Security Officer (CISO) may report to CEO, Board of Directors (BOD), CFO or CIO (Chief Information Officer). While in the past CISO often reported to CIO ... more recently the CISO often reports directly to CEO, CFO or BOD.

Workforce Security

The Workforce security standard is about implementing policies and procedures to ensure that all members of the workforce have appropriate access to PHI, and to prevent those workforce members who do not have access from obtaining access to PHI. The implementation specifications are as follows for this standard:

- Authorization and/or Supervision §164.308(a)(3)(ii)(A) (Addressable) - is about implementing procedures for the authorization and/or supervision of workforce members who work with PHI or in locations where it might be accessed.
- Workforce Clearance Procedure §164.308(a)(3)(ii)(B) (Addressable) - is about implementing procedures to determine that the access of a workforce member to PHI is appropriate e.g. role based access. Periodic (e.g. annual) access review helps prevent "access scope creep" e.g. when people change positions within the organization.
- Termination Procedures §164.308(a)(3)(ii)(C) (Addressable) - is about implementing procedures for terminating access to PHI when the employment of a workforce member ends or as required by determination (audit/review). Comparing user access list with current payroll list is a simple and often used check (control) during audit.

These implementation specifications can be addressed by policies and procedures clearly describing access procedures, stating who can have access to PHI, which job classifications or professional roles are permitted to work with PHI, what are the criteria or professional certifications required; what is the process for verifying employee or business associates information, credentials, employment history, background checks; who makes final hiring and termination decisions for all employees and contractors.

Since these implementation specifications are addressable, the covered entities or business associates have necessary flexibility to implement policies, procedures and tools to meet the standard.

Information Access Management

The Information access management standard is about implementing policies and procedures for authorizing access to (ability or the means necessary to read, write, modify, or communicate) PHI that are consistent with the applicable requirements. The implementation specifications are as follows for this standard:

- Isolating Health Care Clearinghouse Functions §164.308(a)(4)(ii)(A) (Required). If a health care clearinghouse is part of a larger organization, the clearinghouse must implement policies and procedures that protect the ePHI of the clearinghouse from unauthorized access by the larger organization.
- Access Authorization §164.308(a)(4)(ii)(B) (Addressable) - is about implementing policies and procedures for granting access to ePHI, for example, through access to a workstation, transaction, program, process, or other mechanism.
- Access Establishment and Modification §164.308(a)(3)(ii)(C) (Addressable) - is about implementing policies and procedures that, based upon the entity's access authorization policies, establish, document, review, and modify a user's right of access to a workstation, transaction, program, or process.

These implementation specifications can be addressed by policies and procedures clearly describing access procedures, stating who can have access to systems containing ePHI, which job classifications or professional roles are permitted to access ePHI, approve ePHI changes or process specific transactions; who grants, supervises, modifies and terminates the access, what are the conditions and timelines for access terminations or modification and how these actions are documented; how users are uniquely identified and monitored; who grants remote access to organization systems, networks or data; who grants use of personal mobile devices (PMD), and whether PMD agreements are necessary.

Security Awareness and Training

Security awareness and training is about implementing security awareness and training program for all members of its workforce (including management). The implementation specifications are as follows for this standard:

- Security Reminders §164.308(a)(5)(ii)(A) (Addressable) - are about providing periodic security updates. This can be accomplished through periodic trainings, activities or newsletters focused on information security, sharing common pitfalls and promoting security best practices.
- Protection from Malicious Software §164.308(a)(5)(ii)(B) (Addressable) is about procedures for guarding against, detecting, and reporting malicious software. Periodic emails, newsletters can be used to share phishing examples and promote safe behaviors like never turning off the anti-virus or anti-malware software. The procedures should be reinforced with proper device security settings not allowing users to bypass or turn off systems' security features.
- Log-in Monitoring §164.308(a)(5)(ii)(B) (Addressable) is about procedures for monitoring log-in attempts and reporting discrepancies. Appropriately selected monitoring reports will allow for log-in monitoring and computer security policies should be set up in such a way as to prevent brute force attacks.
- Password Management §164.308(a)(5)(ii)(B) (Addressable) is about procedures for creating, changing, and safeguarding passwords. Password best practices can be shared through newsletters and should be supported by properly set security policies forcing users to use password best practices.

The biggest threats to security in the organization are created by internal users. Some of them act maliciously on purpose and other, non-malicious users are just neglecting common sense security precautions. Increasing security awareness through training and reminders is one of the easiest, least expensive and most effective approaches to improve the security posture of the organization. This is also one the most neglected activities in the organizations and is almost always required in post audit resolution agreements. Emphasize security awareness each October, a National Cyber Security Awareness Month – https://staysafeonline.org/

Security Incidents and Breach Notification Rule

Security incident procedures standard is about implementing policies and procedures to address security incidents. HIPAA defines security incidents as attempted or successful unauthorized access, use, disclosure, modification, or destruction of information or interference with system operations in an information system. (definition at 45 CFR 164.304). HIPAA also identifies breaches as, generally, an impermissible acquisition, access, use, or disclosure under the HIPAA Privacy Rule that compromises the security or privacy of the protected health information. (definition at 45 CFR 164.402). HHS guidance indicates that ransomware attack can be a reportable data breach see Ransomware Fact Sheet.

https://www.hhs.gov/sites/default/files/RansomwareFactSheet.pdf

The implementation specification is as follows for this standard:

- Response and Reporting §164.308(a)(6)(ii) (Required) - is about steps for identifying and responding to suspected or known security incidents. The procedure shall identify security incidents, and steps to determine incidents resulting in violations and/or data breaches; how to mitigate, to the extent practicable, harmful effects of security incidents that are known to the covered entity; and how to document security incidents, investigations and their outcomes.

The organization policy shall identify examples of security incidents. The most common security incidents include:

- data/equipment theft or loss
- unauthorized access or use of PHI, inadvertent email distribution
- unauthorized use of system for processing or storing PHI (cloud)
- policy violation (e.g. password/ access sharing)
- inappropriate use of media/social media
- malicious code, virus or hacking incident (ransomware)
- changes to system hardware, firmware, or software characteristics without the owner's knowledge, instruction, or consent (e.g. software downloads)

Not all security incidents result in data breach, but every security incident shall be reported to Security Official and properly documented. The Security Official shall determine if security incident resulted in policy or rule violations and/or data breach using structured, thorough investigation and/or forensic team as needed. Depending on the incident and its severity appropriate actions will be determined by the Security Official or data breach response team. Sanction policy shall be invoked when security incident is caused by employee. Charts below identify process, steps and basic criteria for determining reporting obligations of security incidents, but each incident is unique – document it diligently.

Use decision chart and templates when responding to Security Incidents *(SimpleVCO document - eSECURITY_INCIDENT_RESPONSE.xlsx)*

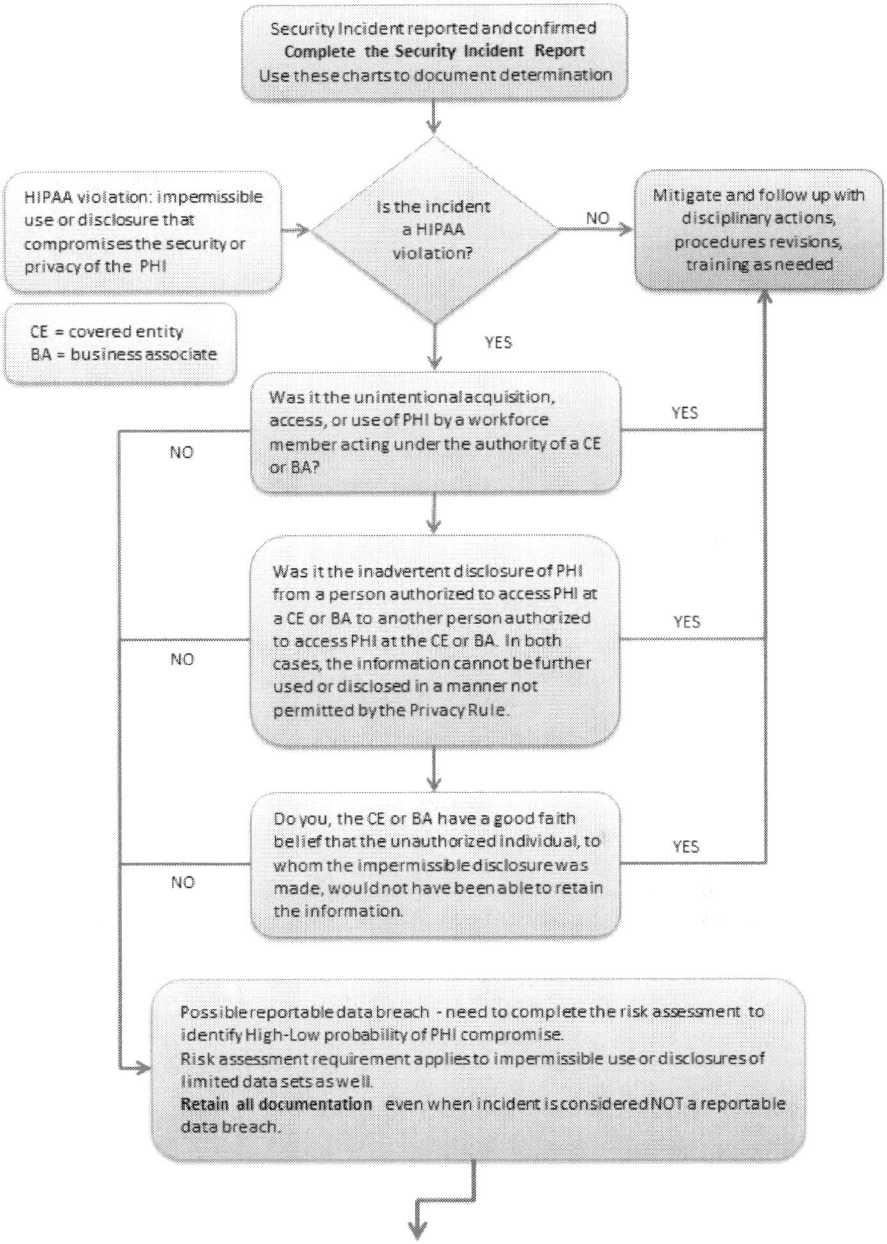

Special attention shall be exercised in regard to incidents resulting in possible data breaches – <u>all incident decision supporting documentation</u> (is it a breach, report or not report, notification etc.) needs to be retained.

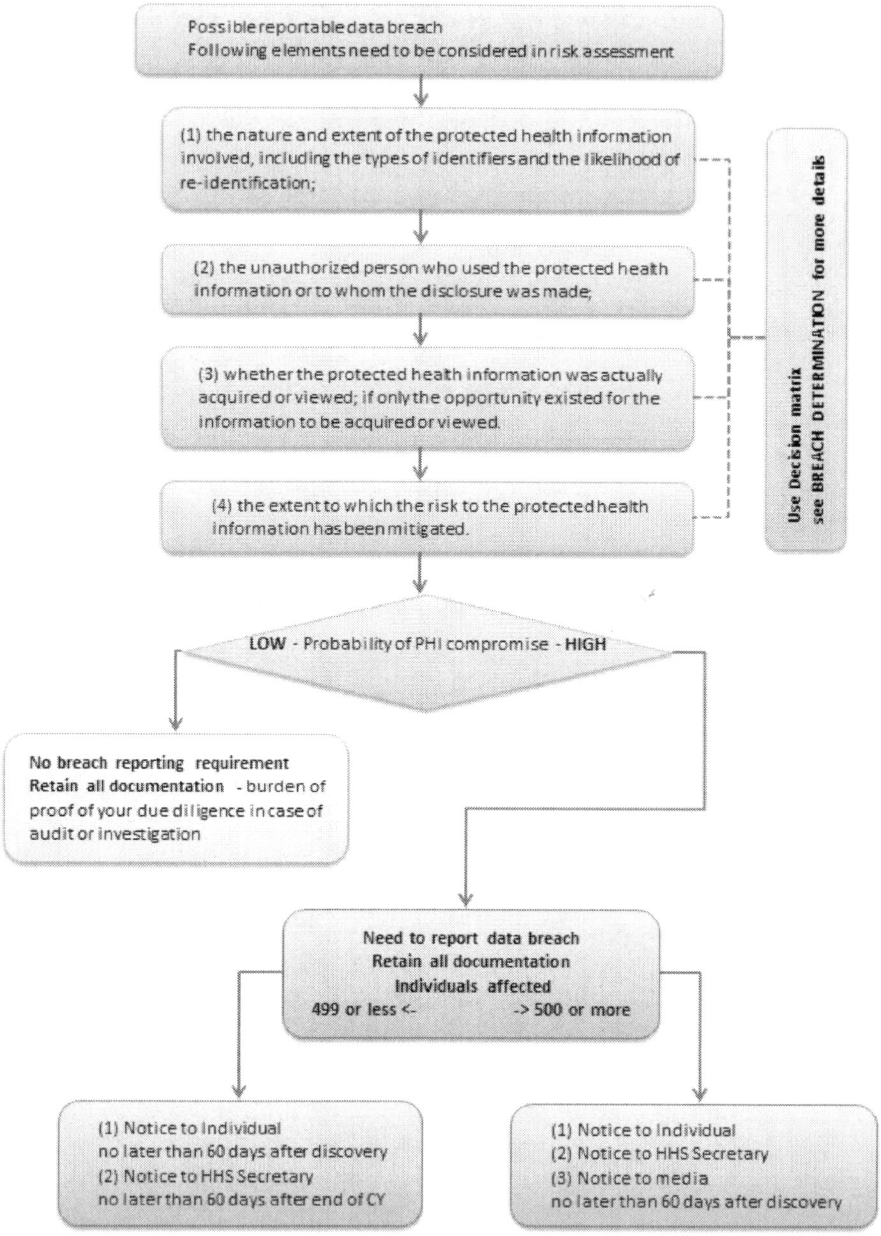

The chart above refers to Decision Matrix - does the breach need to be reported? Because each incident is unique, additional detail needs to be considered – more detailed guidance is provided in Federal Register /Vol. 78, No. 17 / Friday, January 25, 2013 /Rules and Regulations - page 75-78. Pay attention to the business associate (BA) agreements and BA's responsibilities related to incident reports resulting in data breaches.

It is helpful to complete a security incident response evaluation after the incident resolution to identify the positive and negative response aspects and improve future response approach.

Documenting (briefly) even small incidents may help understand and improve end user awareness training and/or security configuration.

- **Breach Notification requirements** 164.404(c) and 164.404(d) - are about timelines for notifications, who and how needs to be notified and what should be included in the data breach notification notice. The chart above identifies timelines and who needs to be notified. OCR provides good instructions on notification requirements and Submitting Notice of a Breach to the Secretary through online portal: http://www.hhs.gov/hipaa/for-professionals/breach-notification/index.html

  Following a breach of unsecured protected health information covered entities must provide notification of the breach to affected individuals, the Secretary, and, in certain circumstances, to the media. In addition, business associates must notify covered entities that a breach has occurred.

  - **Individual notifications** must be provided without unreasonable delay and in no case later than 60 days following the discovery of a breach and must include, to the extent possible, a description of the breach, a description of the types of information that were involved in the breach, the steps affected individuals should take to protect themselves from potential harm, a brief description of what the covered entity is doing to investigate the breach, mitigate the harm, and prevent further breaches, as well as contact information for the covered entity.
  - **Substitute notice** is required when CE has insufficient or out-of-date contact information for 10 or more individuals. Substitute notice has to be provided via web posting or major print or broadcast media, the notification must include a toll-free number for individuals to contact the covered entity to determine if their protected health information was involved in the breach.
  - **Media Notice** is required for data breaches affecting more than 500 residents of a State or jurisdiction (in addition to individual notifications). Media notice has to be provided to prominent media outlets serving the State or jurisdiction. Covered entities will likely provide this notification in the form of a press release to appropriate media outlets serving the affected area. Like individual notice, this media notification

must be provided without unreasonable delay and in no case later than 60 days following the discovery of a breach and must include the same information required for the individual notice.

- **Notice to the Secretary** - In addition to notifying affected individuals and the media (where appropriate), covered entities must notify the Secretary of breaches of unsecured PHI. Covered entities will notify the Secretary by visiting the HHS web site and filling out and electronically submitting a breach report form.
  https://ocrportal.hhs.gov/ocr/breach/wizard_breach.jsf?faces-redirect=true
  If a breach affects 500 or more individuals, covered entities must notify the Secretary without unreasonable delay and in no case later than 60 days following a breach. If, however, a breach affects fewer than 500 individuals, the covered entity may notify the Secretary of such breaches on an annual basis. Reports of breaches affecting fewer than 500 individuals are due to the Secretary no later than 60 days after the end of the calendar year in which the breaches occurred.
- **Burden of Proof -** Covered entities and business associates must be able to demonstrate that all required notifications have been provided or that a use or disclosure of unsecured PHI did not constitute a breach. This section also requires covered entities to comply with several other provisions of the Privacy Rule with respect to breach notification. For example, covered entities must have in place written policies and procedures regarding breach notification, must train employees on these policies and procedures, and must develop and apply appropriate sanctions against workforce members who do not comply with these policies and procedures.
- Similar **breach notification** provisions implemented and enforced by the **Federal Trade Commission (FTC),** apply to vendors of personal health records and their third party service providers, pursuant to section 13407 of the HITECH Act.
  https://www.ftc.gov/tips-advice/business-center/guidance/health-breach-notification-rule

Contingency Plan

Contingency plan standard is about establishing (and implementing as needed) policies and procedures for responding to an emergency or other occurrence (for example, fire, vandalism, system failure, and natural disaster) that damages systems that contain ePHI. The implementation specifications are as follows for this standard:

- Data Backup Plan §164.308(a)(7)(ii)(A) (Required) - is about establishing and implementing procedures to create and maintain retrievable exact copies of ePHI.

  There are three important elements of the backup plan:

  - Backup content and size (files, folders, disk image (OS, software, configuration)),
  - Backup frequency (continuous, daily, weekly) and,
  - Backup location (offsite or onsite).

  Before deciding what to backup an application and data criticality analysis shall be completed (EHR application, ePHI data, billing data, patients' privacy forms, email archives etc.). Backing up applications or creating disk images may speed up recovery process and will help decide about frequency of the backup.

  The size of your backup will impact backup approach and cost. If your critical data changes continuously a weekly backup may not be sufficient to meet your business needs, and technologies like RAID (redundant array of independent disks) or NAS (network attached storage) providing backup redundancy may have to be employed.

  Offsite backup storage is a preferred solution in case a fire or tornado like disaster affects the organization. The organization will have to choose between storing backup devices (drives, tapes) in offsite location and using online (cloud) backup solutions. In both cases it is important to assure the encryption of data in storage devices and/or encryption of data in transmission. It is important to identify in advance the data recovery process and individual responsibilities for assuring data security during recovery process.

  When implementing cloud backup solution make sure your cloud vendor signs the business associate agreement - data storage vendors are business associates!

- Disaster Recovery Plan §164.308(a)(7)(ii)(B) (Required) is about establishing (and implementing as needed) procedures to restore any loss of data or systems functionality.

  - Creating documented disaster recovery plans before disasters occur gives the organization advantage of having a thought through plan of action. Disasters like fire, theft, vandalism, natural disaster, or system (e.g. hard drive) failure are always unexpected and stressful.

- Action plans developed without the elements of stress and urgency, plans developed with team of subject matter experts tend to be better even when they are not 100% applicable to particular situation.
- Disaster recovery plans shall:
    - Consider various disaster scenarios e.g. server theft, fire, water line damage, power failure etc. and how would they affect organization core processes e.g. patient intake and treatment, maintaining Master Patient Index (MPI), issuing birth certificates etc.
    - Identify person responsible for plan implementation and implementation trigger points: who and when starts DRP
    - Contain contact list of staff responsible for specific recovery steps
    - Describe secure data recovery methods and documentation process for lost records
    - Copy of the plan shall be stored outside of the primary business location
    - Implement post disaster management plan, gather feedback, evaluate performance allow for healing process.

- Emergency Mode Operation Plan §164.308(a)(7)(ii)(C) (Required) is about establishing (and implementing as needed) procedures to enable continuation of critical business processes for protection of the security of ePHI while operating in emergency mode.
  The plan shall identify the decision points and decision makers for entering emergency mode operations.
    - Emergency mode operation plan documents multiple emergency mode operations scenarios, documenting processes and alternatives enabling the entity to continue to operate in the event of fire, vandalism, natural disaster, bomb threat, system failure, ransomware, cyber-attack, EHR system outage/unavailability etc.
    - The emergency mode of operations plan shall describe the process for continuing critical business processes like obtaining ePHI during emergency, suspending certain activities, providing emergency assistance to disaster victims, process for emergency access authorization to ePHI, process for disclosing medical emergency to law enforcement, procedures for recovering documents from emergency or disastrous events etc.

  - Include emergency mode operations and disaster recovery in HIPAA security trainings.

- Testing and Revision Procedures §164.308(a)(7)(ii)(D) (Addressable) is about implementing procedures for periodic testing and revision of contingency plans.
  - This can be accomplished through table top exercise, periodic drills and disaster simulations e.g. turning off power to the facility or simulating equipment failure by shutting down a server supporting major function e.g. EHR.
  - Testing procedures should be developed for each contingency plan scenario.
  - The post testing review should reveal the contingency plans' weaknesses, which should be addressed through the plan revisions.
  - Portions of the recovery plans affecting the organization infrastructure (networks, systems) shall be tested every year and the entire disaster recovery plan can be tested every 2-3 years.
- Applications and Data Criticality Analysis §164.308(a)(7)(ii)(E) (Addressable) is about assessing the relative criticality of specific applications and data in support of other contingency plan components.
  - Identifying most critical systems, applications and data will help the organization focus the contingency planning efforts and protect the crown jewels important for organization survival.
  - Focusing on crown jewels also helps in allocating usually limited resources.
  - The assets criticality shall be ranked and valuating the assets may also be helpful in ranking them.
  - EHR, practice management, communications (email), payroll and financial systems are often considered critical to most organizations.

Evaluation

Evaluation standard §164.308(a)(8) (Required) is about performing a periodic technical and nontechnical evaluation of organization security policies and procedures and how they affect the security of PHI. The evaluation will be based on established standards, or in response to environmental or operational changes (e.g. implementing cloud based EHR, moving servers affecting the security of PHI.

The evaluation of policies, procedures and information systems is part of the organization Risk Management Program and shall be conducted as scheduled in Information System Activity Review procedures.

The comprehensive evaluation of organization systems shall be at least conducted annually during completion of the Risk Analysis and development of the Risk Management Program.

Business Associates

Business associate contracts and other arrangements standard is about proper documentation of the business relationship between the organization (covered entity) and contractors creating, receiving, maintaining, or transmitting PHI for or on the covered entity's behalf. The business associate agreement shall provide satisfactory assurances that the business associate/contractor will appropriately safeguard the organization PHI. The implementation specification is as follows for this standard:

- Written contract or other arrangement §164.308(b)(1) (Required) - is about documenting the information protection satisfactory assurances through a written contract or other arrangement with the business associate that meets the applicable requirements of §164.314(a) (discussed later). To meet the standard requirements, the organization should review its contractual business relationships using for example a business associate decision matrix to identify contractors that create, receive, maintain, or transmit PHI for or on behalf of the organization. Vendors providing following services are likely business associates:
    - Claims Processing or Administration (3rd party administrator, a health care clearinghouse that translates a claim from a non-standard format into a standard transaction on behalf of a covered entity (CE) and forwards the processed transaction to a payer)
    - Data Analysis, process, or administration (an independent medical transcriptionist that provides transcription services to a physician, an attorney whose legal services to a health plan involve access to PHI)
    - Utilization Review (a health plan might contract with a hospital to perform their UR, consultant performing UR)
    - Quality Assurance
    - Billing (e.g. external billing, coding service, CPA firm whose accounting services involve access to PHI)
    - Benefit Management (pharmacy benefits manager that manages a health plan's pharmacist network)

- Practice Management, Health Information Organization (HIO/HIE) managing PHI exchange,
- Re-pricing

Other services that may require business associate agreement (when disclosure of ePHI is involved):

- Legal
- Actuarial
- Accounting
- Consulting
- Data Aggregation. See definition §164.501. (Ex: state hospital association, HIE)
- Data storage vendors including cloud storage
- Management
- Administration
- Accreditation -JCAHO, NCAQ, CAP
- Financial Services

Some exceptions from this standard include:

- Disclosures by a covered entity (CE) to a health care provider for treatment of the individual e.g. a hospital is not required to have a business associate contract with the specialist to whom it refers a patient and transmits the patient's medical chart for treatment purposes, physician does not need a business associate agreement with the lab.
- To disclose PHIs to a researcher for research purposes, either with patient authorization or as a limited data. Because the researcher is not conducting a function or activity regulated by the Administrative Simplification Rules, such as payment or health care operations, or providing one of the services listed in the definition of "business associate" at 45 CFR 160.103, the researcher is not a business associate.
- Disclosures to a health plan sponsor, such as an employer, by a group health plan, or by the health insurance issuer or HMO that provides the health insurance benefits or coverage for the group health plan, provided that the group health plan's documents have been amended to limit the disclosures or one of the exceptions at 45 CFR 164.504(f) have been met.
- The collection and sharing of PHI by a health plan that is a public benefits program, such as Medicare, and an agency other than the agency administering the health plan, such as the Social Security Administration, that collects protected health information to

determine eligibility or enrollment, or determines eligibility or enrollment, for the government program, where the joint activities are authorized by law.

While business associates are directly responsible for HIPAA compliance, it is the covered entity responsibility to manage risks related to third parties accessing primary organization networks, systems or data.

Over 20% of healthcare data breaches affecting more than 500 individuals involve business associates; Target and many other large data breaches outside of healthcare - involved partners and contractors - **3rd parties risk management is a must.**

It will be a good business practice for the covered entity to verify prospective business associate status by requesting:

- Certificate of Good Standing
- Documented, 3rd party, independent Risk Analysis
- Proof of professional liability insurance (not just general slip and fall insurance)
- Statement from vendor describing PHI access needs and how the PHI will be handled
- The business associate agreement to be signed by vendor CEO

Physical Safeguards

Facility Access Controls

Facility access controls standard is about implementing policies and procedures to limit physical access to its electronic information systems and the facility or facilities in which they are housed, while ensuring that properly authorized access is allowed. The implementation specifications are as follows for this standard:

- Contingency Operations §164.310(a)(2)(i) (Addressable) - is about establishing (and implementing as needed) procedures that allow facility access in support of restoration of lost data under the disaster recovery plan and emergency mode operations plan in the event of an emergency. The policy and procedures need to identify:
  - Who has the authority to access facilities after hours, and who has the ability to grant emergency access to individuals.
- Facility Security Plan §164.310(a)(2)(ii) (Addressable) - is about implementing policies and procedures to safeguard the facility and the equipment therein from unauthorized physical access, tampering, and theft. The policy and procedures need to identify:

- Which areas can be accessed by guests, and who is responsible for locking the facility, which doors are locked;
- What is the process for reporting theft or tampering with IT equipment;
- Who is responsible for implementation and monitoring of the physical access policies, security video recordings etc.

- Access Control and Validation Procedures §164.310(a)(2)(iii) (Addressable) - are about implementing procedures to control and validate a person's access to facilities based on their role or function, including visitor control, and control of access to software programs for testing and revision. The organization policies and procedures need to identify:
    - What are the sign-in and identification policies;
    - How visitors are identified and controlled within the facility;
    - Who grants and monitors contractors' access to information systems etc.
- Maintenance Records §164.310(a)(2)(iv) (Addressable) - are about implementing policies and procedures to document repairs and modifications to the physical components of a facility which are related to security (for example, hardware, walls, doors, and locks). The organization policies and procedures need to identify:
    - How repairs or modification are documented;
    - How contractors access the facility, and who approves access etc.
    - Contract requirements

Workstation Use and Security

Workstation use standard §164.310(b) (Required) is about implementing policies and procedures that specify the proper functions to be performed, the manner in which those functions are to be performed, and the physical attributes of the surroundings of a specific workstation or class of workstation that can access ePHI. The organization policies and procedures need to:

- Limit the use of systems and equipment for business purposes;
- Emphasize the users' responsibility for exercising good judgment regarding the reasonableness of personal use and limit the use of internet, email, blog or social media during work hours;

- Emphasize the proper use of antivirus or antimalware software;
- Set clean desk policy and limitations on connecting of portable devices and external storage media;
- Set limitations on installing, disabling and uninstalling software;
- Set physical security of workstations preventing shoulder browsing, theft or unauthorized access.

Workstation security standard §164.310(c) (Required) is about implementing physical safeguards for all workstations that access ePHI/PII, to restrict access to authorized users. The organization policies and procedures need to:

- Specify desktop security policy settings like screen saver timeouts, password length and complexity, frequency of changing the password and password history;
- Prohibit unauthorized/unapproved installation of applications;
- Specify requirements for devices encryption (including portable devices);
- Identify use of physical security e.g. cable locks, placement of servers in secure locations;
- Teach users about precautions they need to implement when using portable devices in public places, build security awareness.

These policies should be supported with appropriate computer security settings (device hardening) and use of biometric readers shall be considered to strengthen and simplify workstation security.

Device and Media Controls

Device and media controls standard §164.310(d)(1) is about implementing policies and procedures that govern the receipt and removal of hardware and electronic media that contain electronic protected health information into and out of a facility, and the movement of these items within the facility. The implementation specifications are as follows for this standard:

- Disposal §164.310(d)(2)(i) (Required) – is about implementing policies and procedures to address the final disposition of ePHI, and/or the hardware or electronic media on which it is stored. The organization policies and procedures shall specify disposal methodologies for Protected Health Information (PHI) in non-electronic (e.g. paper, film) or electronic format, and/or the hardware or electronic media on which it is stored. The information shall be disposed of and/or erased in such a way which makes the PHI unreadable and unusable, this is called the sanitization process. The sanitization and disposal shall be documented.

- Paper, photo negatives or CD/DVD documents can be shredded or burned.
- Internal or external electronic storage devices (hard drives, USB drives, memory cards) can be physically destroyed by pulverizing, breaking or cutting, degaussing/demagnetizing, overwriting with non-sensitive data or wiping with other approved methodologies.
- Deleting data and re-formatting drives is not a sufficient method to erase/clear electronic media.

• Media Re-use §164.310(d)(2)(ii) (Required) is about implementing procedures for removal of electronic protected health information from electronic media before the media are made available for re-use. The organization policies and procedures shall:

    - Specify that before reusing electronic media containing ePHI e.g. reusing backup drive containing unencrypted ePHI, selling PC containing ePHI to an employee after PC reached its useful life, the media/devices shall be sanitized. This step shall be documented.
    - Further use of removable media (external hard drives, USB drives) shall be restricted to only organization issued encrypted removable media. Use of third party removable media shall be prohibited.

• Accountability §164.310(d)(2)(iii) (Addressable) is about maintaining a record of the movements of hardware and electronic media and any person responsible therefore. The organization policies and procedures shall require that upon acquisition, re-assignment or disposal of information system equipment, appropriate entries, updates are made in the inventory system to keep track of equipment, media, users and ePHI.

• Data Backup and Storage §164.310(d)(2)(iv) (Addressable) is about creating a retrievable, exact copy of electronic protected health information, when needed, before movement of equipment. The organization policies and procedures shall require creation of a retrievable, exact copy of ePHI, as needed, before movement or disposal of equipment or media. The location of the backup shall be recorded.

Technical Safeguards

Access Control

Access control standard is about implementing technical policies and procedures for electronic information systems that maintain ePHI to allow access only for those persons or software programs that have been granted access rights as specified in §164.308(a)(4). The implementation specifications are as follows for this standard:

- Unique User Identification §164.312(a)(2)(i) (Required) - is about assigning a unique name and/or number for identifying and tracking user identity. To meet these requirements all users shall be assigned a unique identifier (User ID/password) allowing for the information system to log and track users' activity.
- Emergency Access Procedure §164.312(a)(2)(ii) (Required) – is about establishing (and implementing as needed) procedures for obtaining necessary ePHI during an emergency. The organization policies and procedures shall identify individual(s) who can create/ assign user ID/provide access to ePHI in emergency situations.
- Automatic Logoff §164.312(a)(2)(iii) (Addressable) - is about implementing electronic procedures that terminate an electronic session after a predetermined time of inactivity. Automatic logoff feature shall be enabled on all systems providing access to or containing ePHI, when applications do not have this capability a device logoff can be used.
- Encryption and Decryption §164.312(a)(2)(iv) (Addressable) – is about implementing a mechanism to encrypt and decrypt ePHI. Device encryption (e.g. hard drive encryption) and/or file level encryption shall be used as applicable. Encrypting data in transit is addressed in §164.312(e)(2)(ii) Transmission Security.
    - FIPS (Federal Information Processing Standard) compliant device and/or data encryption shall be incorporated to protect ePHI and sensitive data.
    - Devices/data to be encrypted need to be identified, user need to be trained and encryption keys have to be back up.
    - Special attention needs to be placed on encryption of mobile devices, where whole disk encryption shall be used to prevent data breaches and avoid data breach notification. Device encryption shall be documented.

Audit Controls, Integrity and Authentication

Audit controls standard §164.312(b) (Required) is about implementing hardware, software, and/or procedural mechanisms that record and examine activity in information systems that contain or use ePHI e.g. operating system audit and log policies, application event logs.

Systems containing ePHI will have the system activity logging/tracking features enabled, when these features are available. The audit logs will be reviewed as identified and scheduled in the Risk Management Plan and information system activity review schedule. Automation of log capture and analysis is strongly recommended.

Integrity standard §164.312(c)(1) is about implementing policies and procedures to protect ePHI from improper alteration or destruction.

- Mechanism to authenticate electronic protected health information §164.312(c)(2) (Addressable) - is about implementing electronic mechanisms to corroborate that ePHI has not been altered or destroyed in an unauthorized manner. Data verification and reconciliation approaches can be used to assure data integrity and to authenticate ePHI:
    - Encrypted, time-stamped and redundant data backup can be maintained
    - File(s) hash signatures are recorded and verified
    - Billing transactions can be reconciled on a monthly basis

Person or Entity Authentication standard 164.312(d) (Required) is about implementing procedures to verify that a person or entity seeking access to electronic protected health information is the one claimed.

Password policy and unique user identification shall be strictly enforced. Users will be held accountable for all actions performed on the system with their User ID. Biometric readers shall be phased in when feasible to strengthen and simplify authentication process. Multi-factor authentications (MFA) shall be used for remote access, for system administration activities and for access to critical systems.

Transmission Security

Transmission security standard §164.312(e)(1) is about implementing technical security measures to guard against unauthorized access to ePHI that is being transmitted over an electronic communications network. The implementation specifications are as follows for this standard:

- Integrity Controls §164.312(e)(2)(i) (Addressable) are about implementing security measures to ensure that electronically transmitted ePHI is not improperly modified without detection until disposed of. Using data protection tools like digital signatures based on digital certificates, encryption, rights management services (RMS), password protection for documents will assure data integrity.

- Encryption §164.312(e)(2)(ii) (Addressable) is about implementing a mechanism to encrypt ePHI whenever deemed appropriate. The above standard can be met by using secure transmission protocols (https) incorporating current Transport Layer Security (TLS) technologies, encrypting content during transmission with rights management services, digital certificates and S/MIME or other encryption technologies. Public Key Infrastructure (PKI) (digital certificates) is sometimes used in larger organizations. Stand-alone (e.g. ZSentry, ZixMail) or integrated (e.g. Office 365 encryption and Information Rights Management (IRM) in Office 365 Enterprise) solutions provide easy to use file (in transit) encryption capabilities. IRM (also referred to as RMS) applies data protection policy and encryption to a protected file at the same time allowing for access permissions and content expiry management.

Organizational requirements

Business Associate Contracts or Other Arrangements

- Business associate contracts or other arrangements standard §164.314(a)(1)(i) (Required) is about implementing business associate agreements and assuring their content meets specific requirements.

The standard requires that if a covered entity knows of an activity or practice of the business associate that constitutes a material breach or violation of the business associate's obligation, the covered entity must take reasonable steps to cure the breach or end the violation. And if such steps were unsuccessful:

- Terminate the contract or arrangement, if feasible; or
- If termination is not feasible, report the problem to the Secretary.

Violations include the failure to implement safeguards that reasonably and appropriately protect PHI. The contract or other arrangement must meet specific requirements described below.

- Business associate contracts §164.314(a)(2)(i) (Required) requires that the contract between a covered entity and a business associate must provide that the business associate will:
    - Implement administrative, physical, and technical safeguards that reasonably and appropriately protect the

confidentiality, integrity, and availability of the PHI that it creates, receives, maintains, or transmits on behalf of the covered entity;

- Ensure that any agent, including a subcontractor, to whom it provides such information agrees to implement reasonable and appropriate safeguards to protect it;
- Report to the covered entity any security incident resulting in data breach of which it becomes aware;
- Authorize termination of the contract by the covered entity, if the covered entity determines that the business associate has violated a material term of the contract.

- Other arrangements §164.314(a)(2)(ii) (Required) provide additional flexibility in accomplishing the objectives of the business associate agreements.

Requirements for group health plans standard 164.314(b)(1) is about group health plan obligations to ensure ePHI are appropriately safeguarded by plan sponsor when ePHI is created, received, maintained, or transmitted to or by the plan sponsor on behalf of the group health plan.

The plan documents content requirements are similar to the content of business associate agreements listed above.

Policies and Procedures and Documentation Requirements

Policies and procedures standard 164.316(a) (Required) is about implementing reasonable and appropriate policies and procedures to comply with the standards, implementation specifications, or other requirements of the regulations. The standard permits the policies and procedures to be changed at any time, provided that the changes are documented and are implemented in accordance with regulations. The implementation specification is as follows for this standard:

- Documentation 164.316(b)(1) (Required) is about:
  - Maintaining the policies and procedures in written (which may be electronic) form; and maintaining a written (which may be electronic) record of the actions, activities, or assessments required by policies and procedures. To implement this standard, it is essential to organize the folder structure for document storage and retention. Adopting standardized folder or document naming approaches across the organization and dating documentation will make the process easier. This will simplify response to audit requests or investigations.
  - Time limit. Retain the required documentation for 6 years from the date of its creation or the date when it last was in

effect, whichever is later. Incorporating date in document name may help with organizing and retention of documentation.

- Availability. Make documentation available to those persons responsible for implementing the procedures to which the documentation pertains. Assuring easy access to policies and procedures (for reference, to lookup procedure), forms and templates will improve staff compliance and productivity.
- Updates. Review documentation periodically, and update as needed, in response to environmental or operational changes affecting the security of the ePHI. Policies and procedures effectiveness will improve as they are frequently updated. Including effective and revision dates on policies and procedures will help the organization stay organized and in compliance.

There is a certain level of truth in saying: "...if it is not documented, it did not happen". Documenting your risk mitigation or disciplinary actions, system monitoring and staff training efforts will protect your organization. You may not be perfect in all your efforts, but the documentation will help you explain reasoning, decision making and your due diligence.

When dissecting, communicating and operationalizing cybersecurity I find most helpful:

- NIST Cybersecurity framework (Identify, Protect, Detect, Respond, recover) - for developing IT/security strategy and;
- Center for Internet Security 20 Critical Security Controls - for operationalizing IT/Security strategy.

These frameworks are easy to understand and conceptualize, and can be used to build solid security programs, that will help you meet compliance objectives.

Chapter 4 - HIPAA Privacy and Security Risk Management Implementation - Preparing for Audit

Overview

The Risk Management Program implementation process described in this book has been divided into steps to be completed during approximately 25-30 days cycle. The first "round" of Risk Management activities may take longer than the subsequent efforts, depending on the current status of the organization audit preparedness. The completion of the process will establish fundamentals for the risk management program and prepare the organization for compliance audits by creating or initiating necessary processes and activities, and providing necessary supporting documentation. When starting from scratch 1-2 hours each day may be needed for reading and implementing the process. Subsequent risk management maintenance and update efforts should take much less time as they would become part of the familiar business process, and most of the organization documentation, processes, policies and procedures will be in place. Responding to auditor's request for information should be quite straightforward as necessary documentation will be organized and easily accessible.

! The book contains screenshots or examples of necessary or recommended documents. Please visit **www.bizwit.us** to take advantage of the online tools for risk analysis, risk management and privacy and security awareness training. These tools are available on a subscription basis and you can request the toolset demo, we'll be happy to explain, walk you through the SimpleVCO Virtual Compliance Office tools, and assist you to jump start your risk management efforts.

To help navigate through the process and to keep track of task completion it is important to create a time line. Project Management software or a simple Excel spread sheet for smaller organizations may be used. In this book the DOCUMENT_MASTER_INDEX.xlsx serves a dual purpose. It is aligned with the Chapter 4 content to provide a quick reference point, and it allows for development of a simple project management timeline. The document can be used as a primary navigation, follow up tool and a reference point – here are its headers:

TIMELINE	LEAD NAME	TARGET DATE	REVIEWED	COMPLETED	**RELATED DOCUMENTS**	**TEMPLATE LOCATION => FOLDER**	ACTIVITIES & COMMENTS

When creating or updating documents please make sure you update the revision date (usually in the footer of the document) and business name when necessary. **Formalizing** documents means including the latest revision date and signing documents, so they become official, can be and are communicated to associates, and are enforced. Draft documents would "not count" in audit situation.

There are following major milestones in the implementation instructions below:

- Identify and formalize Security (and Privacy) Officials
- Organizing documentation and templates (creating templates)
- Complete Risk Analysis (includes multiple milestones)
- Complete Privacy documents
- Complete Policy and Procedures documents (includes multiple milestones)
- Train staff and complete confidentiality and policy acknowledgement statements
- Implement Risk Mitigation Plan developed during Risk Analysis

Risk Analysis

Process and documentation (Day 1 – Day 5)

Day 1

Step 1

Formalize designation of the Security Official by completing and signing the Security Official designation e.g. Attachment A in Chapter 6 Policies and Procedures example, or by updating position description and clearly stating the Security Official role/ responsibility. Make sure the Privacy Official is also identified and formalized - these roles are often combined.

Security Official will be responsible for development and implementation of Risk Management in the organization. If you have identified Security Official in the past make sure that you save a copy of the document in your current RISK ANALYSIS folder. In small practice the practice owner can be the Security Official, and practice manager can be a backup Security Official. The reversal of the roles can also work well. It is in the best interest for the owner and the manager to be well versed in privacy and security requirements. The specific responsibilities of the Security Official can be modified as needed.

Following responsibilities typically fall under the Privacy/Security Official:

- Ensuring privacy and security policies, procedures, and standards are in place and adhered to by entity.
- Providing basic privacy and security support for all systems and users.
- Providing on-going employee privacy and security education.
- Performing periodic audits/ log review/ risk analysis.
- Managing system(s) users and overseeing information use.
- Reporting regularly to the Covered Entity leadership on entity's status with regard to HIPAA Privacy and Security Compliance.
- Managing Release of Information (ROI) process (privacy role)
- Managing business associates agreements

! These responsibilities need to be added to individual's position description document if those are maintained in the organization.

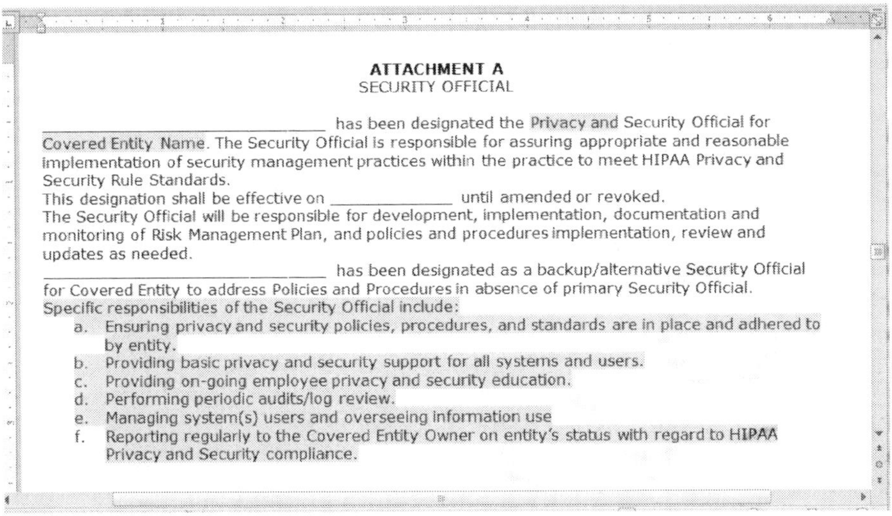

ATTACHMENT A
SECURITY OFFICIAL

_________________________ has been designated the Privacy and Security Official for Covered Entity Name. The Security Official is responsible for assuring appropriate and reasonable implementation of security management practices within the practice to meet HIPAA Privacy and Security Rule Standards.
This designation shall be effective on ____________ until amended or revoked.
The Security Official will be responsible for development, implementation, documentation and monitoring of Risk Management Plan, and policies and procedures implementation, review and updates as needed.
_________________________ has been designated as a backup/alternative Security Official for Covered Entity to address Policies and Procedures in absence of primary Security Official.
Specific responsibilities of the Security Official include:

a. Ensuring privacy and security policies, procedures, and standards are in place and adhered to by entity.
b. Providing basic privacy and security support for all systems and users.
c. Providing on-going employee privacy and security education.
d. Performing periodic audits/log review.
e. Managing system(s) users and overseeing information use
f. Reporting regularly to the Covered Entity Owner on entity's status with regard to HIPAA Privacy and Security compliance.

Security Official designation - ePOLICY_and_PROCEDURES - ATTACHMENT A

Security Official will have to spend some time studying the process and leading others through the steps of risk analysis, development and implementation of Risk Management. Company owners / leadership need to recognize the additional responsibilities and time commitment and allocate time and resources for that.

<u>Step 2</u>

Security Official will **set up folder structure** on designated PC to create and organize framework for further efforts.

Create a RISK_MANAGEMENT folder on your PC e.g. in Documents folder. Suggested folder structure and naming principles will help you organize the documentation and will help with version control.

Helpful TIP

Keep in mind that the Risk Analysis (Assessment) is a snapshot view of your privacy and security efforts. The Risk Management documents will be frequently used for Risk Analysis purposes. These documents will be saved in the Risk Analysis folder with date at the end.

Here is the suggested folder/subfolder structure to organize your Risk Management efforts and documentation:

- 1-RISK_ANALYSIS_DOCUMENTS
- 2-PRIVACY_DOCUMENTS
- 3-POLICY_and_PROCEDURES_DOCUMENTS
- 4-CONTINGENCY_PLANS_DOCUMENTS
- 5-BUSINESS _ASSOCIATES_DOCUMENTS
- 6-BREACH_RESPONSE_DOCUMENTS
- 7-CONTRACT_DOCUMENTS
- 8-HELPERS
- DOCUMENT_MASTER_INDEX.xlsx

The above basic folder structure will help you keep the documents organized and easy to find. This structure is also used in the DOCUMENT_ MASTER_INDEX to create reference points and to help you find appropriate templates etc. Additional subfolders can also be added to the main folder structure. When you create additional subfolders you should add them to the MODULES tab (worksheet) in the DOCUMENT_MASTER_INDEX to help others understand the folder structure and to help them find documents quickly.

The RISK_ANALYSIS_*DATE* folder will contain annual Risk Analysis files e.g. RISK_ANALYSIS_2016. The documents for the following annual Risk Analysis will be saved in newly created folder – e.g. RISK_ANALYSIS_2017.
It is a good practice to add the date at the end of a folder or document to distinguish it from documents completed earlier.... This helps with document version control.

Helpful TIP

To control versions of various document's use date or version number at the end of document.

The 1-RISK_ANALYSIS_DOCUMENT folder shall contain the following:

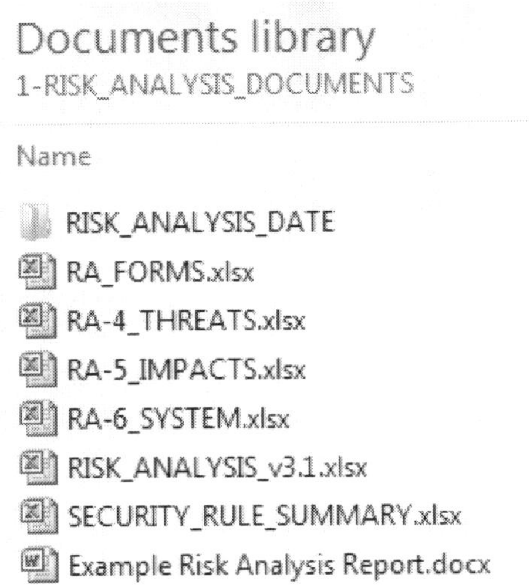

Upon completion of these (and other) documents, you will place them in the RISK_ANALYSIS_DATE folder

These initial steps, and in fact all of the steps from this chapter, need to be completed regardless of the risk analysis tool used. Use the same risk management approach when utilizing Bizwit LLC SimpleVCO toolset, ONC Security Risk Assessment SRA tool, ISACA Risk Register approach or any other risk analysis tool.

Step 3

Create the DOCUMENT MASTER INDEX.xlsx (Excel document project plan in RISK_MANAGEMENT folder) and Save As the DOCUMENT_MASTER _INDEX_DATE in the RISK_ANALYSIS_DATE folder and use this document as your main reference point – documentation and activities roadmap for others to follow as well.

Use the steps from this Chapter to create timeline and project plan. When using SimpleVCO use STEPS tab as the project management tool with start and end dates, tasks and individual responsibilities (if working with the team). This document can be used to frequently review progress of your project and to identify/follow up on TO DO tasks.

Step 4

The SECURITY_RULE_SUMMARY.xlsx is a short version of standards /requirements and implementation specifications pulled from HIPAA Omnibus rule (in 1-RISK_ANALYSIS_DOCUMENTS folder). The document gives a good overview of the HIPAA Security rule standards and implementation specifications. The Risk Management steps, policies and procedures address these exact standards to address healthcare privacy and security, and to meet regulatory compliance. You should create something similar based on Chapter 3 if not using SimpleVCO.

Step 5

Complete the WALK_THROUGH, which is a periodic audit protocol/checklist for facilities physical security and staff adherence to policies e.g. look for written passwords, screen saver & clean desk policy enforcement, PHI in trash cans, locked cabinets, locked windows and doors etc. The WALK_THROUGH audit form will also be used for monitoring purposes during the year.

Helpful TIP

To copy the entire worksheet (tab) right click on the worksheet name (tab name), select "Move or Copy", from "To book" menu select "(new book)" and put check mark in the box by "Create a copy", click OK.

Save the new Excel book (spreadsheet) as: NEW NAME.xlsx

You may actually ask the Security Official backup (if designated) to complete this task unannounced, within certain timeframe to capture an objective picture. **After hours (or during lunch) walk through audits are recommended.**

WALK_THROUGH.xlsx

	A	B	C	D	E
1	DATE:			AUDITOR NAME:	
2	CRITERIA	YES CIRCLE RESPONSE	NO CIRCLE RESPONSE	RESOLVE BY DATE	FOLLOW UP - NAME
3	Are computers shut down/logged off?	YES	NO		
4	Do computers automatically time out, is the screen saver enabled?	YES	NO		
5	Do screen savers use "On Resume, display Log On screen"?	YES	NO		
6	Was there any PHI/PII in trash cans, recycling bins or on the desk?	YES	NO		
7	Are locked shred bins available in the area?	YES	NO		
8	Are back doors locked? Is the router room locked?	YES	NO		
9	Was PHI/PII (reports, lab results, PHI copies on paper or CD) accessible to visitors (on counters, desks, in distribution bins)?	YES	NO		
	Are computer screens with ePHI/PII				

WALK_THROUGH

Example of WALK_THROUGH audit form

Day 2

The documents to be completed in Day 2 can be found in SimpleVCO 3-POLICY_and_ PROCEDURES_DOCUMENTS => eRM_FORMS folder. Not all documents are used for risk analysis tasks, some documents are used during risk management activities. Examples are shown below - some documents may be used by larger entities, or those with more mature security programs. Tasks below focus on covering basics.

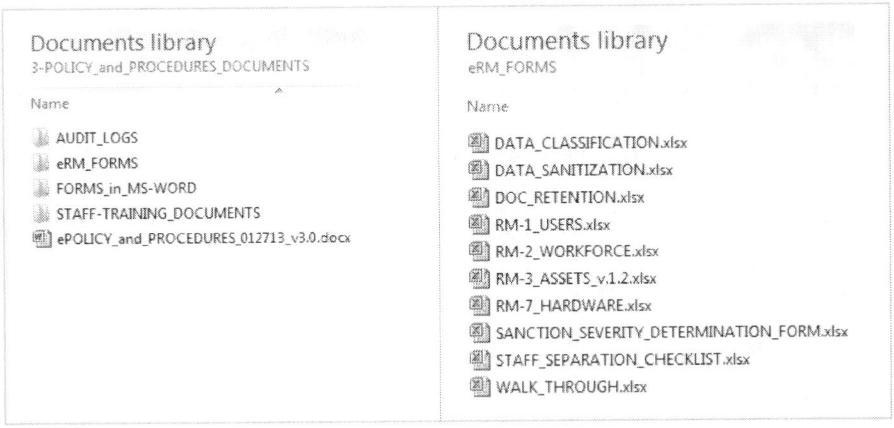

<u>Step 1</u>

Complete the RM-2_WORKFORCE which should list all employees, volunteers and contractors. This is your **people inventory**.

If you are creating this list for the first time, use the eRM_FORMS document as your master list, which you will be updating on a continuous basis. For the Risk Analysis purpose copy the RM-2_WORKFORCE worksheet (after entering all information) to Risk Analysis folder.

The document contains employee contact information, address, confirmation of signed confidentiality agreement on file, access to ePHI, who granted access to systems containing ePHI, last documented HIPAA training, professional certifications, equipment assignments, system access and termination etc. For contractors listing include type of relationship (is it business associate), type of access to your data and type of services provided. Most likely you already have this info in various systems or documents ...The worksheet will keep the information in one place and can replace or eliminate need for some other documents.

Depending on the organization systems and infrastructure appropriate reports may have to be generated to meet the human assets "inventory" objective. Organizations should be prepared to generate following reports for audit, risk analysis or investigation purposes: listing of terminated employees, new hires, network and system administrators, backup operators, privileged users, users with access to ePHI, contractors and vendors with access to ePHI including users' access rights, users with remote access capabilities, organization charts for IT department. Security and access reports from applications (EHR or PM), active directory etc. may be used to produce required documentation and verify proper user and user access management.

In audit, user's list is often compared to current payroll list - to verify termination and access review policies and procedures effectiveness.

Step 2

Complete the RM-3_ASSETS which should list your **organization critical assets, including data assets:** information systems containing sensitive data (e.g. EHR, billing system, network shares, ERP, HR/employee systems etc.), applications, devices where critical and sensitive data is stored. A short description for each asset, IP address/ location, ports opened, external access and data connections, info describing the information they contain or services they provide, how they relate to other assets, and their criticality should be included. For the Risk Analysis purpose copy the RM-3_ASSETS worksheet to Risk Analysis folder.

The Assets document will help prioritize information systems or resources based on their criticality to the organization or sensitivity of the information they contain. This information will be useful when developing risk mitigation plan, updating contingency plans and allocating limited resources. People (contractors) are also part of the **asset criticality analysis.** This document also allows the organization to list location of PHI or sensitive information, who has access to it, and whether it is encrypted or accessed remotely. While this information may be available in other documents, looking at it in this context will help understand better any potential vulnerabilities and may facilitate better actions, it will provide better documentation in case of the data breach investigation.

! Knowing where sensitive data is, helps identify best ways to protect it.

Step 3

Gather **hardware and software inventory**, use automated tools when possible. For very small organizations template RM-7_HARDWARE can be used. If you are creating this list for the first time, use it as your master list, which you will be updating on a continuous basis. Copy the RM-7_HARDWARE to Risk Analysis folder.

The inventory info should include technical information about the equipment for example Computer Name, Domain/ Workgroup, Manufacturer, Operating System and version, System Version, serial number, information about system encryption, age of the system, disposal date, user accounts on the device, drives/ storage etc. SimpleVCO template allows you to score security of the PCs as well. Some automated tools also provide "device health" scoring functionality and allow you to pull the data frequently - thus recommendation for automation.

Software inventory helps identify obsolete, vulnerable or unapproved software, it also helps manage software licensing.

It is also a good practice to include the network/system diagrams, location of wireless access points, firewalls, routers and switches – this gives better understanding of systems design, safeguards put in place and potential weak points. In smaller organizations the information might be readily available, though a certain level of computer skills would be required e.g. navigating through Control Panel in Windows OS.

Automation of inventory processes is highly recommended.

Day 3

Step 1

Complete the RA-4_THREATS document (1-RISK_ANALYSIS_ DOCUMENTS folder), which should list common threats for your organization and the frequency of their occurrence. The threats include natural disasters (flood, tornados), power outages, burglary, hardware, network or software failures, internal or external unauthorized access. Save the document after completion in Risk Analysis folder with appropriate date at the end.

You will use this document when developing risk mitigation plan. While threat frequency may be used as secondary factor in deciding whether to Accept, Defer or Mitigate security vulnerabilities, it may help you understand better the severity of certain vulnerabilities and what are the most appropriate actions to address them e.g. through contingency plans.

	FREQUENCY BASED CRITERIA FOR THREAT LIKELIHOOD	HIGH	HIGH	MODERATE	MODERATE	MODERATE	LOW	LOW	LOW	LOW	LOW
	ANNUALIZED FREQUENCY	365	52	12	4	2	1	0.5	0.2	0.1	0.05
THREATS	THREATS-QUESTIONS \ EVENTS FREQUENCY	Daily	Weekly	Monthly	Four Times Per Year	Two Times Per Year	One Time Per Year	Once Every Two Years	Once Every Five Years	Once Every 10 Years	Once Every 20 Years
NATURAL DISASTER	Is your office in an area prone to natural threats like tornados, fires or floods? How often any of these events occur?							X			

Step 2

Complete the RA-5_IMPACTS document (found in 1-RISK_ANALYSIS_ DOCUMENTS folder), which should list impact categories and their significance on your organization. The Low, Medium and High impact categories will depend on the size of your organization, its revenues etc. and will reflect organization / leaders **risk appetite (tolerance).**

For larger SMB organizations $50,000 cost of identity protection may be considered a Low impact, while for other smaller entities it may be categorized as Medium impact. The figures in the document should be adjusted to reflect characteristics of each organization. A consensus building approach, Delphi technique can be used to categorize impacts.

The threat impacts can be grouped in following categories:

- Reputation/customer confidence, competitive advantage
- Financial (cost of response) and productivity
- Safety and health (employees / patients)
- Fines and legal penalties

Save the document in Risk Analysis folder with appropriate date at the end e.g. RA-5_IMPACTS_2016.

The IMPACT estimates are subjective and fiscal leadership/owner(s) consensus will be helpful in developing this document. In addition, leadership/owners' involvement in this task may be helpful in helping them better understand the business risk related to privacy and security. This may be beneficial when you ask for resources or investment in risk management e.g. justifying PC upgrades, obtaining independent 3rd party risk analysis or incorporating biometrics.

Frequency of scenario (number of times per year)	0 N<= 0.01	1 0.01<N<=0.1	2 0.1<N<=1	3 1<N<= 10	4 10<N<=100	5 100<N
Comments on frequency						
Impact of scenario on business	0	1	2	3	4	5
1. Productivity	Revenue Loss Over One Year					
Impact Rating	I <=0.1%	0.1%< I <=1%	1%< I <=3%	3%< I <=5%	5%< I <=10%	10%< I
2. Cost of response	Expenses Associated With Managing the Loss Event					
Impact Rating	I <=10K$	10K$< I <=100K$	100K$< I <=1M$	1M$< I <=10M$	10M$< I <=100M$	100M$< I
3. Competitive advantage	Drop in Customer Satisfaction Ratings					
Impact Rating	I <= 0.5	0.5< I <= 1	1< I <=1.5	1.5< I <=2	2< I <=2.5	2.5< I
4. Legal	Regulatory Compliance - Fines					
Impact Rating	None	I <=100K$	100K$< I <=1M$	1M$< I <=10M$	10M$< I <=100M$	100M$< I

Impacts matrix example

Another risk analysis approach (used mostly in larger organizations) is to use e.g. ISACA Risk Register format to identify specific threats, risk scenarios and impacts when developing Risk Response.

Step 3

Every organization will have at least one or two major systems (applications) providing access to or using ePHI, or other sensitive data e.g. HR or payroll. It is prudent to analyse these systems security as well.

Complete the RA-6_SYSTEM - this document identifies your systems' e.g. EHR or PM vulnerabilities in areas of password controls, security administration, activity logging, networking and compatibilities. If your EHR and PM systems are separate, you need to complete separate analysis for each system. Use vendor resources if available or ask vendor for help with documenting application/ system security.

Helpful TIP

Most of the Excel documents are not suitable for printing. For documentation purposes it is best to save all documents in respective folders and then burn them to the CD as the Risk Analysis documentation. When deciding to print some documentation please make sure that page formatting meets your needs – adjusting margins, selecting specific print areas and scaling pages helps with achieving the desired outcomes.

When the ERH system is on ONC list of certified products list, retain certification proof and verify product configuration meets security requirements described in RA-6_SYSTEM.

Use http://oncchpl.force.com/ehrcert/CHPLHome to check product certification status.

Identifying specific system vulnerabilities will help you communicate these issues to system vendor, who might be able to address those through updates/upgrades.

Look for independent verification of systems / application security (for non-EHR systems) e.g. independent audits, GRC reports, approvals for use by government organizations, independent or self-attestation at e.g. Cloud Security Alliance STAR registry https://cloudsecurityalliance.org/

Because not all ONC certified or approved systems were created equal, when selecting new systems similar assessment may be helpful in system selection and in identifying approaches simplifying your compliance responsibilities. Knowing system(s) vulnerabilities is also important to allow you to develop additional security layers to address the system vulnerabilities.

For example, if the system does not enforce specified password length and complexity, you need to address this system weakness through your policies and procedures, and enforce e.g. 8-12 characters long password policy through PC security policy.

Day 4

Step 1

The SimpleVCO Risk Analysis Questionnaire is a set of 70 questions mapped to HIPAA Privacy and Security Rules implementation standards. These questions help assess the organization privacy, security and compliance posture and provide a visual, dashboard like perspective.

You can also use 152 questions ONC Security Risk Assessment SRA tool https://www.healthit.gov/providers-professionals/security-risk-assessment - to document your review or other tools.

The RISK_ANALYSIS – (SimpleVCO or ONC SRA tool) questionnaire.

To complete the RA-8_ASSESSMENT questionnaire, you have to have a fairly broad knowledge of systems and processes in your organization. You may need help of your IT professional with answering some questions about IT systems or settings. Ask others for help with answering questions as needed – do not guess answers. **Describe vulnerabilities or issues in Comments** field, you will use these comments when completing the RA-9_RISK_PROFILE. It takes about 60 - 120 minutes to answer all questions describing environment, processes, policies and practices within your organization. This questionnaire provides core information for risk analysis. It is used in conjunction with other information to create the risk profile for your organization and to determine best mitigation strategies.

The risk assessment is not a 30-minutes activity. **First** – It is impossible to capture the complexity of systems and regulatory requirements in 20 - 30 questions. **Second** - Keep in mind that auditors are looking for your company demonstrated due diligence efforts.

Third - it is about your business ... sugar-coating and skimming the surface will not help. The process also helps you build security and risk awareness.

Step 2

When using SimpleVCO tools the HOW_TO tab provides additional instructions on working with the information and Pivot Table summaries in RISK_ANALYSIS document. Start the review and analysis process of the information you collected. Verify that all questions have been answered and refresh all Pivot Tables in the RISK_ANALYSIS document. Use dashboards on the EX_SUMMARY and PT_SUMMARY worksheets to understand specific issues.

Helpful TIP

The risk analysis tasks use the Excel Pivot Tables functionality. To refresh Pivot Table select/click on any cell within the Pivot Table (cell B10) and right click on it => Select refresh from the menu and the Pivot Table values will be refreshed.

Day 5

Step 1

Complete the RA-9_PT_RISK_PROFILE worksheet (in the RISK_ANALYSIS document) to identify specific vulnerabilities, mitigation actions, responsibilities. Use the HOW_TO guidance to pin point system weaknesses. The Risk Profile is directly tied to the HIPAA Standards to clearly address the security, privacy and regulatory compliance requirements, and how the organization is meeting them (or not).

Focus on vulnerabilities identified by "red stop lights", copy and combine vulnerabilities descriptions from RA-8_ASSESSMENT comments field in appropriate column in RA-9_PT_RISK_PROFILE. When looking at specific vulnerabilities you may need to look at other documents already completed e.g. RA-6_SYSTEM, WALK_ THROUGH review or specific hardware vulnerabilities. These additional documents may provide a better insight into potential security vulnerabilities and will help you determine appropriate approach/action.

When addressing specific vulnerabilities look at the potential impacts those vulnerabilities could have on your organization and categorize them as High, Medium and Low, and then check risk mitigation action you think would be most appropriate for specific risk: accept, mitigate / reduce, or defer / avoid / transfer.

The comprehensive look at all this information will help you decide whether the risks need to be mitigated, deferred or accepted. Some risk management practitioners will also talk about risk transfer where an organization purchases insurance to transfer the risk to insurer. Please keep in mind that **insurance (risk transfer) does not mitigate the risk** per se. The insurance can be used to minimize financial impact when the risk is accepted or when the risk cannot be fully mitigated.

Keep in mind this equation:

Total Risk - Mitigated Risk - Transferred Risk - Insurance = Residual Risk Never = 0

When considering cyber insurance, it is important to:

- Fully understand the cyber insurance coverage and exclusions;
- Understand that **completing risk analysis and minimizing critical risks** is first step to obtaining reasonable insurance;
- Understand that implementing specific risk mitigation strategies should minimize your risks and lower the insurance costs;
- Understand that insurance will not cover negligence e.g. lack of encryption or risk analysis; and that your risk exposure will never be equal to 0;
- Some cyber insurance applications will ask about security certifications (CISSP, CISA etc.) of individual's leading your security program or risk analysis efforts.

! Prioritize risk mitigation activities based on their impact and cost. Focus on high priority risk mitigation activities. Keep in mind that the most effective approach to information security is a layered approach.

When using ONC SRA tool review the report and highlight the areas of biggest risks to be addressed in your risk mitigation plan, report summary in the narrative format would be helpful as well to draft mitigation plan.

VULNERABILITY AREAS	Total	VALUE
Access and Audit Control	7	7
Device and Media Controls	1	1
Facility Access Controls	2	2
Information Access Management	2	2
Privacy	5	5
Security Awareness and Training	6	6
Security Management Process	13	13
Security Policies and Procedures	10	10
Workforce Security	3	3
Workstation Security	2	2
Grand Total	**51**	51

SimpleVCO RISK_ANALYSIS - Executive Summary dashboard view

After completion of the RISK PROFILE summarize the analysis results in Risk Analysis Report Narrative

If the particular vulnerability requires technical solution which is not available yet or is too expensive, consider hardening security of other components of your system, implement appropriate policies and procedures, and train staff to minimize the related risk.

In SimpleVCO document RISK ANALYSIS (RISK PROFILE worksheet)- answering additional questions (cost, support needed, ownership) related to **mitigation activities** will help you better understand the effort and its potential cost, which may be a deciding factor in how or if the security gap is addressed.

Helpful TIP

When developing risk mitigation plan or strategies, keep in mind that when e.g. addressing system vulnerability directly is not cost effective or possible, a layered or policy based approach may offer a solution.

When you complete this section, the RA-9_PT_RISK_PROFILE - RISK MITIGATION PLAN for your organization will be completed. This plan will allow you to address privacy and security vulnerabilities. Some of these vulnerabilities may require IT investment or support, and some can be addressed by implementing proper policies and procedures, training etc.

! Remember that technology is not a sole answer to information security, and neither are policies and procedures. *Security is a management issue that may require a technical solution – Shon Harris CISSP.*

Keep in mind that only a coordinated approach will help you create and implement adequate, reasonable and cost effective security measures to prevent data breaches, to protect patients' privacy and to mitigate the business risk.

Refer to your Risk Mitigation Plan as you progress through this manual frequently to complement, and to align policies and procedures with appropriate technology solutions. Entire risk assessment documentation will likely be requested during audits.

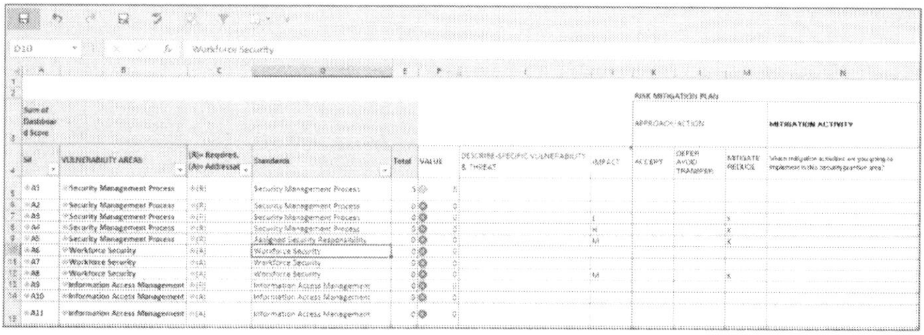

RA-9_PT_RISK_PROFILE - RISK MITIGATION PLAN Worksheet

<u>Step 2</u>

Summarize the analysis results in Risk Analysis Report Narrative – this document is for senior managers, Board of Directors and other decision makers - make it understandable and avoid techno jargon. This document needs to support your message about privacy and security compliance posture and **resources needed to improve it - sign the report.**

Schedule and complete an "Audit Exit conference" (risk analysis update meeting) with senior management, to **present the results of the risk analysis**. This will formalize presentation of the risk analysis results, an opportunity to educate management about issues, and an opportunity to obtain resources and **management support** - the most important factor! Present a summary of next steps/ actions as well.

Day 6 - HIPAA basic awareness training

Step 1

Lack of HIPAA awareness and security training has been identified as one of the most common shortcomings in multiple complaint investigations and audits. Training is also considered to be the most effective and cost efficient method of improving security posture and HIPAA awareness. Entire organization shall complete the HIPAA Awareness training and obtain the certificate of completion or other form of documentation. Group or web based training approaches will give organization and staff necessary level of flexibility - use SimpleVCO training module/ resources, or use ONC training resources including videos and Cybersecurity games found at healthit.gov

Training agenda and copy of the certificate of training completion, or attendance list should be saved in STAFF-TRAINING_DOCUMENTS folder in 3-POLICY_and_PROCEDURES_DOCUMENTS, and appropriate note should be made in RM-2_WORKFORCE to reflect current training completion. This documentation will likely be requested during audits.

Risk Management

After completion of the Risk Analysis tasks, it is time to implement the Risk Mitigation strategies identified in the RISK MITIGATION PLAN (RA-9_PT_ RISK_PROFILE). The steps/guidance below identify tasks that will help you meet all regulatory compliance standards and elements of the HIPAA Omnibus Rule. Following through the policies and procedures allows for the risk mitigation activities to be implemented and aligned with proper documentation. Some organizations may already have certain elements of risk management in place and may use this guidance as a verification or improvement tool for existing practices, policies and procedures. The Risk Mitigation activities addressing security gaps identified in Risk Analysis (RA-9_PT_RISK_PROFILE) should be implemented in collaboration with IT staff.

! It is important to communicate with IT staff clearly to identify best and most efficient technical solutions addressing security gaps, and to **implement technical controls that support organization policies**. It is equally important to coordinate, communicate and align policies and procedures related to technical aspects of security efforts.

Privacy Rule Policy and Documents (Day 7 – Day 8)

Day 7 - Privacy Rule Policy and Documents

Step 1

Lack of updated Notice of Privacy Practices (NPP), updated privacy forms and lack of availability of these documents for patients is one of the most common issues affecting small and medium size providers.

The Notice of Privacy Practices templates included in SimpleVCO toolset provide a comprehensive coverage of patients' privacy rights, descriptions and examples of lawful disclosures... it covers what is required and needed. The brochure format can be easily printed and made available for patients in the office. You can also use http://www.hhs.gov/hipaa/for-professionals/privacy/guidance/privacy-practices-for-protected-health-information/index.html

Review (in Chapter 6) **and update Section XII Privacy** in the ePolicy and Procedures document, and **privacy forms templates** in SimpleVCO folders 3 and 2 respectively).

Update the business name in the Notice of Privacy Practices (brochure format) document, **print it and display it in your organization**. If your organization maintains the website the same Notice of Privacy Practices (NPP) should be posted on your web site. Make sure staff is familiar with patient's rights and NPP.

Do not add patient acknowledgement /consent of financial responsibility to pay the bills to the Notice of Privacy Practices.

Helpful TIP *To make changes in MS Word documents, you can use the Find and Replace feature of MS Word. Find and Replace function is under File/Home menu. Type "PRACTICE NAME" in the "Find what" field and type "Your Practice Name" in the "Replace with" field ... Click Replace all. You will receive a confirmation of how many replacements have been completed.*

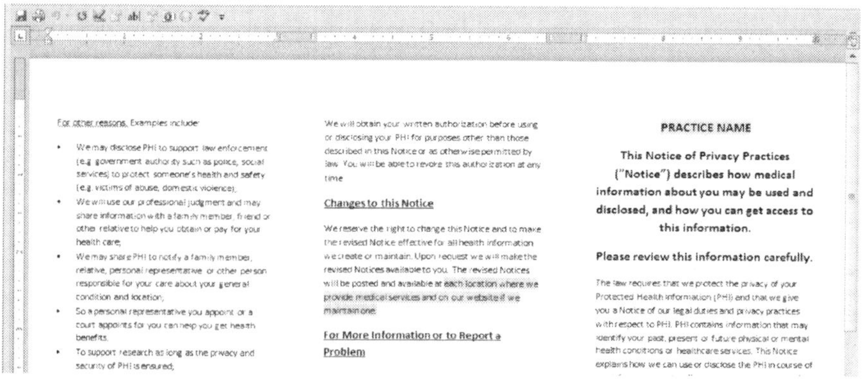

For other reasons. Examples include:

- We may disclose PHI to support law enforcement (e.g. government authority such as police, social services) to protect someone's health and safety (e.g. victims of abuse, domestic violence);
- We will use our professional judgment and may share information with a family member, friend or other relative to help you obtain or pay for your health care;
- We may share PHI to notify a family member, relative, personal representative or other person responsible for your care about your general condition and location;
- So a personal representative you appoint or a court appoints for you can help you get health benefits.
- To support research as long as the privacy and security of PHI is ensured;

We will obtain your written authorization before using or disclosing your PHI for purposes other than those described in this Notice or as otherwise permitted by law. You will be able to revoke this authorization at any time.

Changes to this Notice

We reserve the right to change this Notice and to make the revised Notice effective for all health information we create or maintain. Upon request we will make the revised Notices available to you. The revised Notices will be posted and available at each location where we provide medical services and on our website if we maintain one.

For More Information or to Report a Problem

PRACTICE NAME

This Notice of Privacy Practices ("Notice") describes how medical information about you may be used and disclosed, and how you can get access to this information.

Please review this information carefully.

The law requires that we protect the privacy of your Protected Health Information (PHI) and that we give you a Notice of our legal duties and privacy practices with respect to PHI. PHI contains information that may identify your past, present or future physical or mental health conditions or healthcare services. This Notice explains how we can use or disclose the PHI in course of

NPP_3C_BROCHURE-OCR.docx - NPP in handout format

Step 2

Complete the Privacy forms necessary to document and address patient's rights. Identify business name to be used on the privacy forms and on your Notice of Privacy Practices. When using SimpleVCO open all forms and replace the PRACTICE NAME with your specific business name - use find and replace features of MS Word to simplify and speed up this task.

Update revision date in the footer of the document.

Some forms may require additional modifications (look for red font).

Please make sure that your staff especially front desk staff knows where the privacy documents are, and that they are familiar with them, so they will make them available upon patient request, and so they can assist patients with form completion. Your organization should have following **basic privacy forms**: NPP, patient authorization to disclose PHI, consent for electronic communications, request for access to PHI, request for accounting of disclosures, request for PHI amendment, request to restrict PHI uses and disclosures, request to be contacted at different address, request to designate personal representative and complaint form regarding use of PHI.

If you need to create additional forms, you should use the form template so all your practice forms have the same format and appearance. This will emphasize the practice professional look.

! One of the common information security problems is that organizations collect data that they do not really need. Reviewing data collection needs and **minimizing data collection** is a good step towards minimizing risk exposure. Do not collect more patients' information than you really need to accomplish the task on your privacy forms e.g. stop collection of SSN on every form, if absolutely needed for authentication ask for last 4 digits.

Day 8

Step 1

Covered entities are required to record the provision of NPP to patients/ client. Decide how are you going to meet that requirement (NPP acknowledgement form or log). The simple log approach (log book) is often used by pharmacies. In high patient volume practices this approach may be replaced by electronic signature pad (for NPP acknowledgement), like for credit card transactions, or by entirely electronic intake document completion on tablets. My often recommended approach is to incorporate NPP acknowledgement in patient intake document instead of using another paper form and scanning it.

Your job is to define the process for your practice/ organization, develop template, document it and share it with front desk staff so it is consistently implemented. Capture the procedure in policy and procedures document.

Step 2

Review and complete the document inventory and categorize practice documents as those belonging to the Designated Record Set (DRS) and/or to the Legal Health Record (LHR). The LHR will be used to satisfy formal/legal request for information about individual's PHIs, and DRS will be used to satisfy individual's rights (to obtain, inspect, disclose, amendment and obtain accounting for disclosure of PHIs) described in the HIPAA Privacy rule.

The DOCUMENT INVENTORY - DRS-LHR will make it easier to respond to records requests. Staff can use it to identify which documentation needs to be included in record request for e.g. insurance company and which documentation to include when responding to patient request for e.g. accounting of PHI disclosures. The document inventory will also help you identify where ePHI resides and whether it is adequately protected.

Policy and Procedures

So far we did the risk analysis, we've provided basic privacy/ security awareness training and updated our organization privacy forms. During risk analysis we may have discovered technical system's vulnerabilities (e.g. lack of antivirus on some devices, outdated Java 6 or firewall software, default passwords on network devices etc.) and other issues that need to be addresses ASAP. Let the IT staff know about these issues so they can resolve it quickly, while we can work on policies and procedures or rules of the road so to speak. **Why do we need policies and procedures?** Because nothing happens without the written rule, because we cannot communicate what is expected, and we cannot enforce these expectations, we cannot keep people accountable.

Administrative safeguards (Day 9 – Day 20)

Day 9 - Policy development

Step 1

Review Chapter 6 (or ePOLICY_and_PROCEDURES template when using SimpleVCO) to create and/or update your policies and procedures. The template we make available through SimpleVCO includes policies and procedures in one document. We took this approach to increase the document usability, we do NOT want this document to be a shelf document used once a year. We want it to be a guide and a reference point for staff, that is searchable (Ctrl+F) and easy to navigate through content links - decide if this approach is acceptable for your organization.

Some sections e.g. acceptable Internet or email use, sanctions etc. may need to be incorporated in employee manual as well (or instead) for larger organizations. This document needs to be signed upon completion and made available to staff. We recommend electronic signature and PDF format to retain search and navigation functionality.

Update definitions, names, effective date. We recommend referencing Privacy and Security Rule "as amended", or referencing HIPAA Omnibus Rule, rather than using HITECH term as the HITECH provisions have been changed in 2013 by HIPAA Final Omnibus (Final) Rule - same applies to your business associate agreement template.

Step 2

Security Management Process – Assign Security responsibilities and Risk Analysis sections – review and update as needed. Scope of Privacy/ Security Official responsibilities can be expanded as needed. Incorporate professional certification requirements (e.g. to meet cyber insurance considerations) and scope/ triggers/ frequency for risk analysis section.

Step 3

Review Risk Management section, confirm responsibility and high level approach. Incorporate additional detail as you refine your risk management, security monitoring over the years as you e.g. automate inventory, vulnerability or indicators of compromise detection.

Day 10 - Security Management Process – (Day 10 – Day 11)

Step 1

Sanction policy – This entire section (or portion of it) may be incorporated in employee handbook – include a reference in security policies. Adjust disciplinary actions as needed and include clear examples of security violations. Communicating these policies and consequences of policy violations is an effective preventive measure. When dealing with security incidents consider if completion of security incident report is needed. This documentation may protect your organization in case of employment related litigation, audit or investigation. Properly documented actions e.g. against individuals acting maliciously will put your organization in better position.

Step 2

Information System Activity Review - This procedure will help you identify reports and logs to monitor and document system(s) activity. Understand the 20 Critical Security Controls https://www.sans.org/critical-security-controls/ and structure system monitoring activities around top 8. While penetration testing has its purpose, for most of the SMBs it should be used after organization security reaches certain level of maturity, and e.g. top 15 Critical Security Controls are managed well.

Firewall, antivirus, system(s) access and inventory reports are often used to monitor system's activity. Your EHR access and/or "transaction" reports would be a good choice as well. Periodic vulnerability and configuration scanning helps uncover networks and systems vulnerabilities.

Investing in continuing monitoring tools and Security information and Event Management (SIEM) shall be considered to consolidate security monitoring and alerting. Modern cloud technologies can be used to create (or outsource) affordable, effective, virtual, one-man Security Operations Centre (SOC) for SMBs.

! The purpose of system activity review is to provide security alerts, identify Indicators of Attack (IoA) and Indicators of Compromise (IoC), to identify policy violations – **to prevent, detect and stop data breaches**.

When identifying tools and reports availability focus on automation – use as few tools as possible, use tools that work well together, and know their full capabilities. While open source, free tools are appealing to many, we only use licensed tools from reputable vendors as they provide level of support and assurance about detection and alerting capabilities. Keep also in mind that many free tools are **free for personal use** – when they are used for business purposes you might be violating copyright laws ... and in litigation situation your due diligence arguments may be weak.

Day 11

Step 1

Identify reports and develop monitoring schedule to log and monitor activities within your organization. Use RM-MONITORING to keep track of system monitoring activities and compliance tasks. Save documentation in 3-POLICY_and_PROCEDURES _DOCUMENTS\AUDIT_LOGS\2016 folder

Helpful TIP

Use MS Outlook or other task/calendar solutions to schedule recurring reminders about tasks, audit log reviews or when specific reports need to be saved and reviewed.

Examples of reports/ audit log reviews should include walk through audits, firewall, end point security audit logs, system and/or PHI access logs, basic scanning, training completion, security incidents detection etc.

Month / System/Log	Jan	Feb	Mar
Hardware and Software Inventory	1.00	1.00	1.00
AV/AM update/incident report	1.00	1.00	1.00
Summary Report	1.00	1.00	1.00
Quarterly Quiz/Training	1.00		
Risk Analysis			
PERCENT COMPLETION	100%	80%	100%

RM_MONITORING (monitoring calendar) provides a dashboard view of monitoring activities and should be reviewed and reported monthly with leadership for any organization. It forces the documented review of the privacy and security related issues and problems in the organization. This report adds the accountability component, as it is an indirect check/verification of following the monitoring schedule and following up, resolving issues. This report should be submitted to the organization leadership periodically, signed off and retained for HIPAA documentation purposes.

Step 2

Based on activities identified in monitoring calendar you may want to create a procedure or template for capturing specific activity logs/reports. A step-by-step approach allows staff to quickly and consistently complete the activity, assure data, reporting and staff training consistency.

Vulnerability scanning or penetration testing reports usually provided by security vendors should be understandable, should identify and prioritize vulnerabilities and provide corrective steps.

Day 12 - Section IV. WORKFORCE SECURITY and INFORMATION ACCESS MANAGEMENT Mobile devices, patient authentication and communications

Step 1

Section IV point A Personal Mobile Devices (PMD) and determine policy for use of personal mobile devices in your organization. This policy is often referred to as Bring Your Own Device (BYOD). Review and modify as needed ATTACHMENT C Personal Mobile Devices Use Agreement.

The use of PMDs is growing rapidly and organizations struggle with management of these devices, as they provide access to or may contain PHI. Thus why, it is important to incorporate PMD device use agreements to clarify users' responsibilities and allowable use of the devices, and to inventory the devices possibly containing your PHI. As additional security measures are implemented the agreements may have to be modified to secure employers' rights in regard to tracking, monitoring and management of these devices.

Make sure that all staff is familiar with the Personal Mobile Devices policy and only approved devices are used for accessing PHI. Avoid storing PHI on PMD unless appropriate safeguards (e.g. encryption) are in place. Pay special attention to proliferation of smartphone apps and their security issues. The PMD include laptops, tablets, smartphones and external drives (including flash drives). Make sure use of all PMDs is documented with the PMD agreements, and all PMDs are inventoried, to provide tracking information in case of device loss or theft.

Use mobile device management (MDM) tools to enforce safeguards for mobile devices (encryption, PINs, screen lock, wipe).

Step 2

Review Section IV Use of PHI data and patient authentication (Minimum necessary rule). Make sure staff understands minimum necessary principle, can identify HIPAA data elements, understands concept of data de-identification, and knows how to address request for PHI - see DOCUMENT INVENTORY Designated Record Set vs. Legal Record Set.

Read and review Section IV.C Patient Authentication and Patient Authentication Procedure (Explain, Verify and Authenticate - EVA). Depending on capabilities of your particular EHR system or office, update organizational procedure as needed.

For example, if your organization decides to take patients pictures during first visit and store them in the EHR, these pictures can be used to authenticate patients during subsequent visits. Creating customized phone scenario for patient authentication (EVA) will establish specific requirements and process and may also be helpful for new employees.

Step 3

Read and review Section IV.D Email, text, web, social media and oral communications. There are ongoing and growing concerns about web spoofing, email phishing, social engineering and evolving social media threats and exposures. Current policies and procedures may have to be amended as technology changes and emerging vulnerabilities are identified. This section may need to be incorporated in employee handbook as well, and shall be frequently addressed in training.

Day 13 – Section IV - Access Authorization, Workforce clearance policy, Termination policy and Access establishment.

Step 1

Determine who will approve and grant access to the organization systems. Incorporate concept of role-based access e.g. only physician can sign or electronically order prescriptions. In larger SMBs create role-based access control matrix to manage system's permissions e.g. nurses have access to specific EHR modules, physicians have access to all EHR modules etc.

Step 2

Determine appropriate steps for workforce (and contractors) background verification and clearance, who will be responsible for background checks, federal or state registries verifications. Make appropriate updates for workforce background check, contact and clearance information, and access authorization or employee termination. Use RM-2_WORKFORCE worksheet located in 3-POLICY_and ... folder to record workforce information in small organizations. Use TERMINATION checklist to account for e.g. timely system access removal, assigned device return.

Maintaining accurate workforce records is important in case of a disaster or a security incident. It is necessary to have the contact information available outside of your practice/office to be able to contact staff in emergency situations. Secure online storage can be used for contingency plans, emergency contact lists etc.

Step 3

Health Care Clearinghouse Functions need to be isolated from Covered Entity functions - this is usually a concern only for large organization, where billing and insurance related functions are performed along healthcare service delivery.

Step 4

Determine who will handle system access establishment and modification for staff. Pay special attention to use of shared credentials (eliminate or minimize), and remote access to systems, especially with elevated privileges (admins). These responsibilities may be shared between Security Officer and system's manager.

Day 14 - Section V. SECURITY AWARENESS AND TRAINING

Step 1

Security reminders are part of building privacy, security and HIPAA awareness. Review policy and identify frequency and sources for security reminders and trainings ... we learn through repetition, so we need to constantly refresh importance of security, privacy and HIPAA compliance. SimpleVCO subscription includes services supporting training and reminders, but you can also use ONC resources, www.staysafeonline.org and incorporate reminders/ training into your staff meetings.

Step 2

Protection from Malicious Software - gateway and/or host based antimalware, antivirus and firewall solutions, anti-exploitation tools like Microsoft EMET are recommended safeguards. System configuration and even Data Loss Prevention (DLP) tools can play a role in protecting organization from malicious software. Identify tools and applicable policies and train users on best practices and how to recognize security incidents.

Step 3

Log-in monitoring and Password Management - review and update. Depending on the use of biometrics in your organization you may need to amend your policies to reflect best practices and give users instructions about how to get the most from the use of biometric readers and related software to ease access while maintaining adequate security. Keep in mind that proper and enforced policy (e.g. PSWD policy) can address certain system/application shortcomings that may be too expensive to implement.

Security policies of the operating system when properly implemented can simplify and strengthen security policies and procedures implementation.

! The policies and procedures can be used to create additional layer of security. The technology by itself, without aligned policies and procedures may not provide sufficient security. The policies, procedures and technology have to be aligned and coordinated to maximize their effectiveness – and staff needs to be trained.

The training certificates or attendance lists are important part of documenting your risk management activities – do not ignore it. These documents are almost always requested during audits.

Use the RM-2_WORKFORCE worksheet (workforce inventory) located in 3-POLICY ...folder to record staff trainings, certifications etc. Save copies of trainings in 3-POLICY ... \STAFF-TRAINING_DOCUMENTS.

Day 15 - Section VI Security Incident Response and Reporting

Step 1

Ability to recognize security incidents and understanding how to react is a first step for effective security incident response – modify policy and procedures as needed, provide common security incidents examples.

6-BREACH_RESPONSE_DOCUMENTS folder contains:

EXAMPLES of data breach notifications

Actual OCR and FTC RESOLUTION AGREEMENTS with various entities

Example layout of 6-BREACH_RESPONSE_DOCUMENTS folder

Step 2

SimpleVCO toolset includes eSECURITY_INCIDENT_RESPONSE document in 6-BREACH_RESPONSE_DOCUMENTS folder. This document outlines steps and provides templates for triaging security incidents, creating Security Incident Report, identifying potential data breaches, determining reporting responsibilities and action steps when dealing with data breach situation (see charts on page 33 of this book). Becoming familiar with these documents will help you recognize and address security incidents properly. Make sure staff understands the topic as well.

When not using SimpleVCO you should create similar documents using ONC, AHIMA SANS or other resources to assure the process and documentation meet rule, OCR and auditor's expectation.

Review documents in 6-BREACH_RESPONSE_DOCUMENTS\ EXAMPLES folder to see how organizations affected by security incidents approached media releases, reporting responsibilities and communication with various stakeholders.

Step 3

Review eDATA_BREACH_COSTS document (page 13 of this book) to understand the consequences of data breach. You can also use this document to **communicate the security risk and cost associated** with it when justifying request for resources. Understanding the cost components of the data breach will help see the return on investment (in data security) more vividly. The benefits of being proactive and making relatively small investments are more apparent when comparing costs of eliminating security vulnerabilities with potential business consequences of not addressing these issues.

Day 16 - Section VI Contingency Plans

Step 1

Review and update Contingency Plan - Data Backup Plan. Modify procedures as backup solutions/technology change, or as you strengthen these procedures in your organization. One way of strengthening the backup plan is to create backup redundancy e.g. supplementing in-house backup with online backup or vice versa - automate when possible.

In SimpleVCO use the eDRP-CONTINGENCY_PLAN template (in 4-CONTINGENCY PLANS DOCUMENTS folder) to develop scenarios and document contingency plans.

! Make sure the backup covers necessary files, is encrypted and offsite, and its frequency meets your business need e.g. if ePHI data changes hourly make sure the backup is continuous.

Step 2

Review and update Contingency Plan - Disaster Recovery Plan (DRP)

While your basic element of the contingency plan: "grab the black box/back up disk and run" seem to protect vital information, in reality it is not enough. Your data will be useless without your EHR, PM or accounting software, your data will not be complete, you may encounter data integrity issues and spend significant amount of time on data synchronization or resolving data errors. Simple plan identifying and **prioritizing recovery of critical systems, DRP triggers** and key decision makers will minimize negative effects (costs) if recovery.

Proper backup and recovery of risk management, tax or financial documents and systems will put your business back on line faster as well.

! Make sure that the copy of CONTINGENCY PLANs and key staff contact information is always stored and available off premises. Review and update contingency plans periodically – system's criticality, technologies, people and phone numbers change.

Use CONTINGENCY_PLAN_TEMPLATE to create Contingency Plans (CP) for various scenarios e.g. WATER_BREAK_CP, EHR_SYSTEM_CP etc. Use CONTINGENCY_PLANS worksheet to mark completed scenarios and to develop new once.

Helpful TIP

Use Excel Data Validation feature and VLOOKUP function to create drop down menu for Disaster type and to automatically populate assumptions/scenario details in CONTINGENCY_PLAN_TEMPLATE. Both features are extremely helpful in many situations when working with Excel.

Day 17 - Section VI. Contingency Plan – Emergency Mode Operation Plan and Contingency Plan Testing and Revisions, Applications and Data Criticality Analysis and Evaluation

Step 1

Review and update Emergency Mode Operation Plan also referred to as Business Continuity Plan (BCP). Identify critical business functions that need to be continued in emergency situation. Identify how PHI will be obtained, who will grant access to PHI in emergency situations etc. Modify procedures as environment/technology change, use scenarios and eDRP-CONTINGENCY_PLAN templates, update emergency contact information frequently in RM-2_WORKFORCE document.

Step 2

For contingency plans testing and revisions select likely to occur scenarios like power or network outage, or water line break, which would be fairly easy to simulate by turning off power or network router. This will allow staff to implement and test/practice alternative procedures...and practice makes you perform better. The disaster recovery and emergency mode of operations plans should be tested/ evaluated annually - use table top exercise or simulation.

You should address Applications and Data Criticality Analysis when reviewing organization assets (RM-ASSETS), and clarify systems/ data prioritization and recovery in DRP and BCP plans: EHR and PM including various sub-systems e.g. ER, communications (phones and email), identity and financials systems are usually critical.

Day 18 Section VI Business Associates Contracts and Other Arrangements

Step 1

Review Section VI Business Associate Contracts and Other Arrangements. Review business associate agreements (BAA) provisions at http://www.hhs.gov/hipaa/for-professionals/covered-entities/sample-business-associate-agreement-provisions/index.html and make sure your organization template, and BAA you receive from others meet the requirements, and understand Business Associates (BA) responsibilities. When you determine that a BAA is needed for particular vendor you can:

- Create a BAA addendum to existing contract;
- Incorporate BAA elements in the new/renewal contract (2016_BA_AGREEMENT_TEMPLATE in SimpleVCO)

Keep in mind that the BA agreements should protect your organization, and that BAAs from large vendors may be "non-negotiable" (non-amendable). In situations like EHR implementation, it might be beneficial to ask Business Associates using your ePHI, to document the ePHI use through BA_DEVICE_REPORT (example in 5-BUSINESS_ASSOC... folder.

! The Business Associates Device Report puts accountability elements in place: who has ePHI, why, how is it protected and destroyed after use etc. While Business Associates are directly responsible for data protection and breaches, 3rd party monitoring puts more emphasis on security of your ePHI and gives you clear understanding of your ePHI vulnerabilities. This is important because you are still responsible for your PHI, and it is about your reputation, potential litigations against your organization and your name in the newspaper.

Step 2

Review eBA_DECISION_CHART located in 5-BUSINESS_ASSOC... folder. Use this chart to determine vendor/contractor status and the need for Business Associates Agreements (BAA).

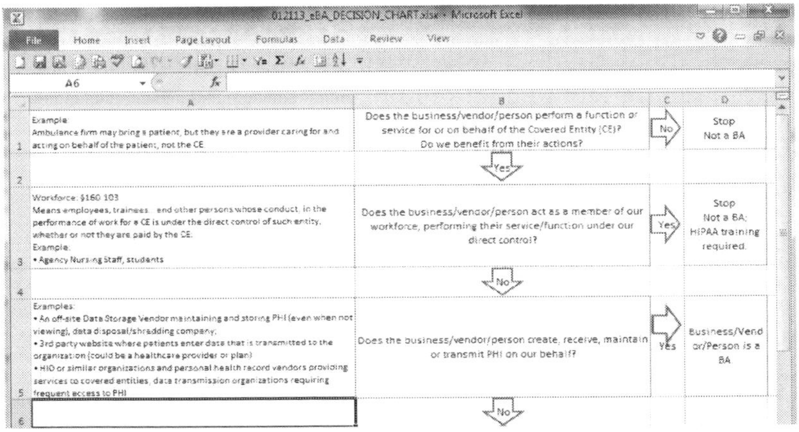

Use RM-2_WORKFORCE to list your contractors and business associates, and to manage BAAs. If not using SimpleVCO create a list that at least contains following information:

Partner Name	BUSINESS ASSOCIATE STATUS	BAA in place	Last BAA date	SERVICES PROVIDED
Mozy	**BA**	**No**		**Cloud Storage**
Clean Jan	**Not a BA**	**No**		**Janitorial Services**

Physical Safeguards

Day 19 - Facility Access Controls

Step 1

Review and update policies for facilities access in emergency or disaster situation - Contingency Operations access. Identify individual(s) allowed to access facility in emergency situations or to implement contingency operations, and assure access control and validation procedures are implementable. Record emergency/contingency access permissions in RM-2_ WORKFORCE document in the COMMENTS field to have it documented and to provide a reference for staff or compliance authorities.

Review and update Facility Security Plan that may incorporate security systems, CCTV, burglary alarms, proximity readers/ card access, sign in sheets etc. Identify the person responsible for locking facility at the end of the business day.

Step 2

Review and update Access Control and Validation, and Maintenance Records Procedures – who can grant access, who can access facilities (e.g. delivery, repairs) and who can access restricted areas like server room, pharmaceuticals or records storage etc. Identify sign in and out process for staff, contractors and visitors, and individuals responsible for granting access. Retain documentation of all facility repairs, maintenance or modifications (what, when, who) especially pertaining to IT/network.

Day 20 - WORKSTATION SECURITY

Step 1

Review and update Section VIII WORKSTATION SECURITY Workstation Use and Workstation Security. It is important to emphasize for staff proper workstation use and applicable use restrictions e.g. Internet and email use for personal purposes, password policies, software downloads etc.

Workstation security may have to be modified to accommodate e.g. your specific biometric solutions, PC characteristics or operating system security policies when used (e.g. password requirements, password change frequency etc.) as described in Chapter 3, Workstation Use and Security section. Minimize your electronic footprint - dispose of unused devices properly, do not let them sit around the office. Coordinate policy development, details and implementation with IT/ security as needed.

Day 21 - Device and Media Controls

Step 1

Review and update Section IX DEVICE AND MEDIA CONTROLS Disposal, Media Re-use and maintain inventory of all devices with automated tools or in RM-7_HARDWARE. The inventory of the devices is one of the simplest and quite effective means of implementing device and media controls, it promotes accountability.

Pay special attention to the use of removable devices e.g. USB flash drives. These devices can be easily connected and can easily store significant amounts of data including PHI. You may consider layered security approach to removable media including disabling USB ports, use of only approved, inventoried and encrypted devices, and strong policy enforcement. Review SANITIZATION_FORM to document proper sanitization, disposal or destruction of devices used in your organization. Retain attestation of device destruction/sanitization especially when it was used to store PHI/sensitive data, include: device description, serial number, sanitization/ destruction method, date, by whom. Remember about contractor's device sanitization or documented data destruction. The business associate agreement should specify what happens with e.g. your PHI after vendor completes the assignment. When using third party for device sanitization make sure you maintain proper documentation.

Step 2

Review and update Accountability, Data Backup and Storage policies. When devices/hardware are decommissioned, make sure data is backup before devices are disposed of.

! Keep in mind that expensive, top of the line firewall and SAS 70 Type II cloud storage is worthless if the back door to your facility is open. Physical security seems to escape attention of small businesses, but it is often the least expensive safeguard to implement, can be a compensating control and it is an essential element of effective layered security approach.

Technical safeguards

Day 22 – Access Control - Unique User Identification, Emergency Access, Automatic Logoff, Encryption and Decryption

Step 1

Review and update policies in Section X Unique User Identification, Emergency Access and Automatic Logoff. These technical controls relate to and enforce safeguards covered in Administrative Safeguards e.g. unique user identification, person or entity authentication etc. these sections refer to devices security configuration that needs to be in sync with policy.

It might be helpful to review again the Workforce Security and Information Access Management Policy, Emergency Mode Operations, Workstation Security, Information System Activity Review, Security Awareness and Training in context of this section.

! The technical access, audit and authentication controls have to support administrative safeguards (policies and procedures) described earlier and vice versa.

Consider use of biometric readers to strengthen and simplify authentication process. Larger organizations may consider implementation of Public Key Infrastructure management (digital certificates for device and/or identity management, and others may consider Office 365 hybrid or cloud based identity management. I recommend Office 365 solution for small organizations and those with mobile workforce, as it provides strong identity management, identity protection, multifactor authentication and has many security tools like data loss prevention, encryption, mobile device management etc. baked into the product, so companies can avoid a "bolt on" security. Professionally configured Office 365 environment provides secure and manageable infrastructure and integrates well with additional security tools like SIEM.

Step 2

Review and update Encryption and Decryption policy and (especially for larger organizations) consider data classification policy. Review how data is transmitted between your organization and vendors. Are secure transmission protocols (https indicating TLS technologies) incorporated, are locked padlocks or "green" web browser address bars indicating secure connections and address validations, are Office 365 Rights Management Services (Information Rights Management) or digital certificates used for signing and encrypting data in transmission.

! Keep in mind that advanced skills and understanding of encryption is required to set up effective use of file level encryption, or to implement whole disk encryption, and backing up encryption keys is essential.

In context of many data breaches resulting from lost, unencrypted devices, and respective calls for encrypting devices, it may be just a matter of time when lack of encryption may be considered negligence. Whole disk encryption is a recommended approach for protecting your data.

Some encryption solutions can be quite transparent for the end users. Remember to document device encryption and reflect device encryption status in the inventory / RM-7_HARDWARE master document. In case of device loss or theft, documented whole disk encryption will provide "safe harbor" exemption from data breach notification requirement, thus eliminating significant costs associated with data breach response.

Using data protection tools like digital signatures based on digital certificates, encryption, password protection for documents will assure data integrity. Regular data backup and periodic transaction reconciliation will help find potential errors and support data integrity.

Day 23 - Audit Controls, Integrity, Person or Entity Authentication, Transmission Security

Step 1

Review and update the Section X Audit Controls, Integrity, Person or Entity Authentication, Transmission Security. When configuring device security e.g. audit controls, follow best practices described by NIST, Microsoft or Centre for Internet Security benchmarks.

Consider cloud solution like Office 365 integrating many useful security features. Use professional help when configuring and implementing these solutions, use partners who have Office 365 competency as it's functionality is much broader, and configuration is different than email Exchange server.

! IT operations will often put emphasis on functionality, speed and ease of access or maintenance of IT systems ... certified security professionals will put emphasis on security and compliance (documentation). Both perspectives are important – your system's configuration needs to balance both elements. Use certified security professionals (CISSP, CISA, CHPS, CISM, GIAC etc.) help.

Organizational Safeguards

Day 24 - Business Associate Contracts, Policies and procedures documentation requirements, retention policy and electronic signatures

Step 1

Review and update Section XI Organizational Safeguards Policies & Procedures Documentation. This section talks about the required content of the business associate agreements (addressed earlier), about the need to maintain version control of policies, procedures and forms, about using the "last updated" or revision date, about record retention policies and about their availability to staff.

All HIPAA related documentation, including Policies and Procedures documents have to be retained for at least 6 years. See SimpleVCO DOC_RETENTION for more record retention guidelines/ schedules.

Including short document retention reminder on templates and documents will be helpful for staff.

Step 2

Review and update Section XI Electronic Signatures. I thought it is important to address this topic as we automate and digitize our business processes.

! In policies and procedures document (Chapter 6 or one available in SimpleVCO), Section XII deals with Privacy Policies. These policies and procedures were addressed during days 7-8, when privacy templates were updated. I suggest short version of the procedure on each privacy form as a quick reference for staff working at the front desk with patients.

! SimpleVCO version of the policies and procedures also includes Section XIII EMPLOYEE STANDARDS OF CONDUCT and ETHICS for small organizations. I often see this as part of employee handbook as well.

Day 25 - Confidentiality statements and policy acknowledgement documentation

Step 1

Review Top 10 Things to remember about HIPAA Privacy and Security with staff and modify as needed. Consider posting it as a best practice in your office. Make sure front desk staff knows where the privacy documents are and is familiar with these forms.

Make sure all staff members know where the Policies and Procedures can be found, they are familiar with it, and have access to these documents at all times. Consider using solutions like SharePoint (part of Office 365 subscription) the make the documents available.

Read and review the ATTACHMENT B - Confidentiality Statement and Policy Acknowledgement. **Provide policies and procedures training to staff.**

One of the possible training approaches might be to ask individuals to review the Policies and Procedures document, and follow up with group training highlighting main topics and creating opportunity to respond to their questions.

After training obtain workforce signatures on the Confidentiality Statement and Policy Acknowledgement. The copy of the document should be saved in the personnel file and appropriate note shall be made in RM-2_WORKFORCE document. Have staff re-sign this document annually as a reminder of the company expectations and possible enforcement - use electronic signatures when possible!

Make Policies and Procedures available to your contractors so they are aware of their responsibilities and your security practices.

Implementing interactive login reminder about organization policies, and forcing users to acknowledge acceptance of company policies and procedures, before accessing the organization systems is another way of strengthening information security and compliance within the organization.

Risk Management continuing effort

Day 26

Review the Risk Mitigation Plan developed during the Risk Analysis process. Verify that all mitigation actions are in progress.

Sign up for a privacy/security awareness/updates newsletter and distribute it to staff regularly/ monthly ...

Set up and follow the monthly Monitoring Calendar and reporting schedule:

- Review and save XYZ reports
- Complete and document staff training
- Re-sign policy acknowledgements
- Review policies and procedures for data backup
- Update disaster recovery plan contact list
- Complete and review vulnerability scans
- ...

Day 335

Have RISK ANALYSIS completed (steps from Day 1 through Day 6) preferably by independent 3rd party reviewer.

As mentioned in the Overview section, because of the technology and regulatory changes, because of the people turnover and new emerging threats, the Risk Management process is an ongoing, continuous effort, which needs to be maintained throughout the year.

Healthcare is not the only area affected by privacy and security challenges. We can learn some best practices from financial, banking and other industries. Sharing examples of best data breach prevention and detection practices, as well as examples of security failures, and penalties or consequences resulting from those failures, helps reinforce the privacy and security awareness among healthcare workforce.

Sharing examples of security incidents and setting relevant examples in your organization works effectively as a preventive measure deterring policy violations, and as you know an ounce of prevention might be worth a pound of remediation.

Examples of innovative and efficient use of new technology solution or workflows will help office managers improve policies and procedures and find better, more efficient and secure ways of doing business every day. Overall they really want to excel at their jobs, and with a little help they will do just that.

Chapter 5 - HIPAA Privacy and Security Awareness

Training and practice helps reinforce specific concepts, rules or behaviours. Most of the mistakes we make are because we do not know what the proper response or action is, because we do not fully understand the consequences, because we have not been in this situation before and because sometimes we just react instinctively. Training and practice will help develop better instincts, better responses and better actions.

There are classroom or web based training solutions available to improve HIPAA Privacy and Security Awareness. The quiz below can be used for training within the organization it is just example of one of the options.

Quiz

HIPAA Privacy and Security Quiz

1	When assessing privacy and security risk in the practice:
A	It is best to use internal staff who knows best how we do business
B	It is best to use 3rd party independent, comprehensive assessment to get objectivity
C	It is best to wait and see because these risks do not affect us
D	It is best to wait for free, official HHS/OCR audit

2	The most efficient and secure way to access PCs in the practice is to:
A	Share one strong password so authorized staff can efficiently access PCs when needed
B	Use unique password for each individual accessing and using particular PC
C	Use biometric (e.g. fingerprint) readers to access PCs
D	B and C

3	When patient calls in and asks for information about lab results it is OK to share those results when:
A	The caller ID shows patient number
B	Patient provides name, address and last four digits of SSN or birth date
C	Patient confirms the name, address and phone number you give to patient
D	You have patient consent to share the data
4	Reviewing firewall and/or network access reports:
A	Is not needed because firewall protects the network
B	Should be handled by specially trained IT staff
C	Would not provide any useful information
D	Should be a part of a Security Official routine
5	When using company PC:
A	It is OK to download applications that increase productivity
B	It is prohibited to install any software without permission
C	It is OK to disregard anti-virus/spyware warnings when visiting familiar websites
D	A and C
6	PC data back up of the patient health information including health records, billing, insurance information:
A	Should be completed daily
B	Is not needed because we have paper files
C	Should be encrypted and stored off site
D	A and C
7	Which of the following events constitute Security incident
A	Unauthorized PHI access or use
B	Data/equipment theft or loss
C	Information Security Policy violation
D	A, B and C
8	What is the best way to address the spill destroying the computer containing PHI?
A	Call trusted IT professional to see if the computer/hard drive can be repaired and data recovered
B	Take the PC to trusted data recovery services to see if PHI data can be recovered
C	Replace the PC and move forward, re-enter data later
D	Follow Contingency Plan and restore data according to Data Backup plan

9	What is the benefit of emergency/contingency planning?
A	Planning mitigates harmful effects of the unexpected
B	Responses are better and quicker as things are thought through before emergency
C	Planned actions are organized and assure PHI protection
D	A, B, and C
10	When laptop with whole disk encryption, containing patient data is lost or stolen we need to:
A	Notify HHS Office of Civil Rights immediately
B	Notify HHS Office of Civil Rights and affected individuals within 60 days
C	Complete the Security Incident report to document loss of encrypted laptop
D	B and C
11	What is the most important factor when applying discipline for privacy and security violations resulting in security incidents?
A	Severity of the violation e.g. cost/level of external exposure
B	Consistency in applying sanctions
C	Employee status/role in the practice
D	Intent of the violator
12	Benefits of having written information security policies and procedures include:
A	Clear and replicable standards and expectations
B	Enforceable and defendable policies documenting due diligence in case of litigation
C	Documented guidance/instructions for training and everyday reference
D	A, B and C
13	When responding to subpoena for Protected Health Information (PHI):
A	The practice should determine specific PHI elements to be released
B	Designated Record Set needs to be provided within 7 days
C	Legal Health Record needs to be provided within 14 days
D	B and C

14	When entering into a contract agreement with vendors you should:
A	Verify vendor status with Secretary of State
B	Avoid boiler plate contract language when possible
C	Determine vendor business associate status
D	A, B and C

15	Which of the following documents are most likely to be requested by OCR/HHS or State Attorney General Auditors?
A	Documented IT systems inventory
B	Security and privacy policies and procedures
C	Recent Risk Assessment and Risk Mitigation plan
D	A, B and C
16	The best practice to protect the privacy of the Protected Health Information (PHI) include:
A	Frequent training about HIPAA Privacy and Security requirements, providers' policies, and providing practical compliance/security reminders.
B	Making staff aware of providers' sanctions policy, monetary penalties for individuals and entities, and criminal sanctions.
C	Implementing policies, procedures and technology solutions for enforcing appropriate safeguards for providers' data, devices and people
D	A, B and C

17	In general, without patient written permission, the patient health information cannot be used or shared:
A	With patients' employer.
B	With any organization for marketing or advertising purposes.
C	For national security purposes.
D	A and B

18	**The Notice of Privacy Policies must be:**
A	Posted in the office
B	Offered to each patient at the first visit after April 14th, 2003
C	Posted on the website if the Practice has the website
D	A, B and C
19	**When patient requests copies of her/his medical records:**
A	They can be charged $0.25 per page
B	They can be charged reasonable cost-based fees, but not exceeding State set amounts
C	They can be charged any fee determined by practice manager
D	They can be charged reasonable cost-based fees, plus 20% for overhead expenses
20	**Patient written consent is necessary for the practice to:**
A	Share patient's medical information when making referral to specialist
B	Post patient picture on Practice website
C	Complete Practice costs accounting analysis for specific treatments
D	Disclose patient's information when sending a super bill
21	**The best way to satisfy HIPAA Privacy Rule compliance requirements is to:**
A	Have patients sign consent form permitting unrestricted PHI disclosure
B	Have patient's rights explained in Notice of Privacy Policies and have appropriate forms available
C	Have all patient consents, requests and authorizations notarized
D	Direct patients to HHS website so they can learn about HIPAA Privacy Rule

22	When patient request medical record amendment it is best to:
A	Explain that medical records can never be amended
B	Explain that the request will be reviewed, and response provided within 60 days
C	Explain that if Practice agrees to amend the record, Practice may ask for contact information for other healthcare providers to notify them about the amendment.
D	B and C
23	HIPAA training should be documented for:
A	Clinical staff working in the Practice
B	Office/support staff working in the Practice
C	Business associates working with the Practice
D	A, B and C
24	The concept of minimum necessary disclosure does not apply to:
A	Disclosure resulting from specific authorization
B	Treatment related disclosures to or by healthcare provider
C	Disclosure made to patient's family
D	A and B
25	Patients can submit complaints about the use or disclosure of their PHI to:
A	Practice Privacy and/or Security Official
B	Office of Civil Rights/Health and Human Services
C	State Attorney General Office
D	A, B and C

26	The maximum Civil Monetary Penalties that can be assessed for willful, negligent and not corrected HIPAA violations can be:
A	$50,000 each violation - Up to $1.5 million, per year
B	$1000 each violation - Up to $100,000 for identical violations, per year
C	$10,000 each violation - Up to $250,000 for identical violations, per year
D	$100 each violation - Up to $25,000 for identical violations, per year
27	The Criminal Penalties for offenses committed with the intent to sell, transfer, or use PHI for commercial advantage, personal gain, or malicious harm are:
A	Up to $100,000 and up to five years in prison
B	Up to $250,000 and up to 10 years in prison
C	Up to $50,000 and one year in prison
D	Up to $200,000 and up to 10 years in prison
28	Updated Data Breach notification rule requires that media, individuals and Secretary of HHS are notified when security or privacy of protected health information is compromised, and when more then _______are affected.
A	250 Individuals
B	750 Individuals
C	500 Individuals
D	1000 Individuals
29	The most effective strategies to protect your data and information systems include:
A	Device encryption
B	Strong and enforced password policies
C	User's access controls
D	A, B and C
30	In course of business, the Practice may need business associate agreement(s) with:
A	Practice employees
B	Practice attorney
C	Cleaning contractor
D	Nurse practitioner providing services in the Practice

31	The most significant costs resulting from data breach include:
A	Legal and defense costs
B	Incident investigation costs
C	Cost of credit monitoring for affected individuals
D	A, B and C

32	What are the major purposes of the HIPAA Act?
A	Protect patients' rights, privacy and safeguard protected health information
B	Implement Insurance Reform and Administrative Simplification rules to provide portability and continuity of healthcare coverage and to improve the efficiency and effectiveness of the health care system
C	Provide healthcare coverage for individuals, provide portability and continuity of healthcare coverage and adopt transaction standards for electronic data interchanges
D	Provide healthcare coverage for individuals, provide portability and continuity of healthcare coverage and reduce administrative costs of nationwide healthcare systems

33	HIPAA Transaction Standards include the following transactions:
A	Claims and encounter information, Payment and remittance advice, Premium payment
B	Claims status, Eligibility, Coordination of benefits, Enrollment and disenrollment
C	Referrals and authorizations
D	A, B and C

34	The federal agency responsible for HIPAA Privacy, Security, Enforcement and Breach Notification Rules enforcement is:
A	Centers for Medicare and Medicaid Services (CMS)
B	National Institute of Standards and Technology (NIST)
C	Office for Civil Rights (OCR)
D	Office of the National Coordinator for Health Information Technology (ONC for HIT)

35	When looking at HIPAA Privacy and Security regulations from regulatory compliance perspective the following should be considered:
A	"Inspiring Confidence and Trust in Health IT" is one of federal priorities
B	Regulatory, non-compliance penalties are high and State and Federal authorities are stepping up enforcement
C	ACO participation may require documented compliance
D	A, B and C
36	The following will assure successful implementation of HIPAA Privacy and Security Risk Management program:
A	The bottom up approach driving best practice implementation from the trenches
B	The top down management support
C	IT professionals should only be involved
D	A and C
37	Implementation of the information security Risk Management program should start with:
A	Review of the best end point security solutions
B	HIPAA Awareness training
C	Completion of comprehensive Risk Analysis
D	Updating information security policies and procedures
38	Which of the following activities are common in the qualitative risk analysis process?
A	Assigning dollar values to assets and calculating annual loss potential
B	Identifying and ranking critical information assets
C	Identifying and ranking threats, vulnerabilities and potential impacts
D	B and C
39	Which of the following activities is not part of the information system activity review?
A	Review of the firewall and end point security reports
B	Review of the EHR system access log
C	Review of the staff benefits utilization
D	The walk-through audit

40	Which of the following is usually not a responsibility of the Security Official?
A	Updating employees contact information and status in the organization
B	Reporting regularly on entity's status with regard to HIPAA Security compliance
C	Providing basic security support for all systems and users
D	Performing periodic audits/log review
41	Security reminders, Protection from malicious software, Log-in monitoring and Password Management are implementation specifications for one to most effective and cost efficient approaches for improving security posture of the organization. Which HIPAA Security standard these specifications refer to?
A	Security Awareness and Training
B	Information Access Management
C	Security Management
D	Workstation Use and Security
42	Which Data Backup plan would be most appropriate for busy primary care practice using practice/server based electronic health records (EHR) system?
A	Backup of the EHR data from the server is completed manually at 5 PM every day to external hard drive
B	Backup of the EHR data from the server and from all PCs is scheduled every other day at 5 PM to Network Attached Storage (NAS) device.
C	Backup of the EHR data from the server and from all PCs is completed continuously to secure offsite location using encrypted internet protocol.
D	Backup of the EHR data from all workstations is completed daily at 5 PM to secure offsite location using encrypted internet protocol.
43	What is the most important element of the Emergency Mode Operation Plan?
A	Periodic testing of the plan.
B	Identifying trigger points and the decision maker for implementing emergency mode operation.
C	Providing sufficient emergency assistance to victims
D	Emergency access authorization to ePHI

44	Which of the following entities is not an example of business associate?
A	Claim processing vendor
B	External billing services company
C	Independent medical transcriptionist
D	Laboratory processing blood test
45	Which of the following elements shall be covered in the Disaster Recovery Plan to make it effective?
A	The plan shall identify person responsible for plan implementation
B	The plan contains contact list of staff responsible for specific recovery steps
C	Copy of the plan shall be stored outside of primary business location
D	A, B and C

46	Which of the following elements are not part of the facility access controls?
A	Sign in sheet for visitors and guests
B	Key card door locks
C	Biometric readers for workstation access
D	After hours security guard

47	Which of the following elements are not part of workstation use and security standards?
A	Limitations on installing, disabling and uninstalling software
B	Password length, complexity, history and change frequency
C	Secure data recovery methods and documentation process for lost records
D	Physical security of workstations
48	Which of the following methods is not acceptable for sanitizing hardware or electronic storage devices?
A	Overwriting with non-sensitive data
B	Deletion and re-formatting
C	Demagnetizing
D	Pulverizing

49	Assigning unique user identifiers (UID) for each user is crucial for:
A	Proper access control
B	Logging and tracking user activity
C	Audit controls and authentication
D	A, B and C
50	Following elements are vital for encryption technology to provide the most benefits:
A	FIPS compliant
B	Whole disk
C	Encryption key backup
D	A, B and C
51	Which of the following is the strongest indication that the internet data transmission is encrypted?
A	Http in the beginning of the web address
B	Https, green address bar in the web browser and locked padlock
C	SSL/TLS protocol
D	McAfee or Symantec Verified label on the website

Quiz Answer Key

Question Number and Correct Answer

1	B	18	D	35	D
2	D	19	B	36	B
3	B	20	B	37	C
4	D	21	B	38	D
5	B	22	D	39	C
6	D	23	D	40	A
7	D	24	D	41	A
8	D	25	D	42	C
9	D	26	A	43	B
10	C	27	B	44	D
11	B	28	C	45	D
12	D	29	D	46	C
13	A	30	B	47	C
14	D	31	D	48	B
15	D	32	B	49	D
16	D	33	D	50	D
17	D	34	C	51	B

Chapter 6 - Policy and Procedures Example

The document below is an example of organization policy and procedures document for healthcare organization. This document is a starting point and framework for developing policies and procedures customized to meet your specific business processes and organizational needs. Forms and templates will give you an idea about documentation necessary for audit purposes, how to streamline data collection or how to better use existing resources. This will ultimately contribute to possibly streamlining some business or reporting processes, better efficiencies and less stress when responding to auditor's request for information.

Parts of this document are shaded to highlight element that need review and modification to reflect your business need. While the document sections are mapped to HIPAA Privacy and Security standards, the components of this document can of course be used for other, non-healthcare organizations, because the HIPAA privacy and security standards are similar to, or are more demanding than standards used in other business sectors.

The Bizwit LLC SimpleVCO subscription provides access to continuously updated documents e.g. policies, procedures and templates as rules, additional rule guidance, technology changes and feedback from our customers help me improve this documentation.

General Operations and Information Security Policies and Procedures

Table of Content of the Policy and Procedures example document

I. <u>POLICY</u>

The purpose of this policy is to define terms, definitions, policies and procedures to assure safe and HIPAA compliant operation for Covered Entity (Organization). The purpose of this policy is to also protect the information related assets including information (software, tools, data) and information systems (hardware and infrastructure).

A. It is the policy of this Covered Entity that Protected Health Information (PHI) and Confidential Information, as defined below, in all its forms--written, spoken, recorded electronically or printed--will be protected from accidental or intentional unauthorized modification, destruction or disclosure throughout its life cycle. This protection includes an appropriate and reasonable level of security over the practice facilities, media, equipment and software used to process, store, and transmit that information.

B. It is the policy of this Covered Entity to comply with all applicable Federal and State standards including but not limited to statutes, regulations and sub regulatory guidance.

C. All workforce members must promptly report loss or misuse of Covered Entity Protected Health Information or Confidential Information to Security Official. All workforce members must conduct themselves in an ethical manner and promptly report issues of noncompliance or any potential fraud, waste and abuse to Compliance /Security Officer.

D. All systems implemented after the effective date of these policies are expected to comply with the provisions of this policy where possible. Existing systems are expected to be brought into compliance where possible and as soon as practical.

E. The scope of this policy includes the protection of the confidentiality, integrity and availability of Protected Health Information (PHI) as defined below in DEFINITIONS, in accordance with HIPAA Privacy and Security Rules, and safe and secure operation of the organization.

F. This policy applies to all Covered Entity Workforce as defined below in DEFINITIONS.

G. This policy applies to Personal Mobile Devices owned by Covered Entity Workforce as defined below in DEFINITIONS.

H. Security Official will be responsible for development, implementation and enforcement of the information privacy and security policies and procedures.

I. Information privacy and security policies will be approved by the executive of the organization.

J. This policy is effective as of DATE

K. This policy has been revised on: DATE

______________________	______________________	____________
Executive name and title	*Signature*	*Date*

II. DEFINITIONS

Terms used, but not otherwise defined, in this Agreement shall have the same meaning as those terms in the HIPAA Privacy and Security Rule.

A. Business Associate is an entity that "creates, receives, maintains, or transmits" protected health information on behalf of a covered entity as described in § 164.308(b) of the Security Rule and § 164.502(e) of the Privacy Rule. Business associate term can only apply to entities conducting function or activity regulated by the Administrative Simplification Rules.

B. Covered Entity. "Covered Entity" shall mean PRACTICE / ORGANIZATION NAME.

C. Confidential information. "Confidential Information" shall mean private or otherwise sensitive information (not classified as protected health information (PHI)) that must be restricted to those with a legitimate business need. Examples of Confidential Information include: personnel information, key financial information, proprietary information about business partnerships, system access passwords, file encryption keys etc.

D. Individual. "Individual" shall mean the person who is the subject of the Protected Health Information.

E. Information system. "Information system" shall mean an interconnected set of information resources used by Covered Entity. A system normally includes hardware, software, information, data, applications, communications, and people.

F. Personal Mobile Devices. Personal Mobile Devices shall mean any devices not owned by the Covered Entity, and able to store, communicate, record or transport ePHI or Confidential Data. Personal Mobile Devices may include laptops, cell phones, smartphones, tablets e.g. iPad's, iPod's, PDAs, any data, video and voice recording devices, external drives including USB/Flash drives and memory cards etc.

G. Privacy Rule. "Privacy Rule" shall mean the Standards for Privacy of Individually Identifiable Health Information at 45 CFR Part 160 and Part 164, Subparts A and E as amended.

H. Protected Health Information. "Protected Health Information (PHI)" shall mean individually identifiable health information that is held, transmitted or maintained in any form or media, whether electronic, paper or oral.

I. Required By Law. "Required by Law" shall mean a mandate contained in law that constrains a use or disclosure of PHI.

J. Security Official. "Security Official" shall mean the person assigned responsibility for assuring Covered Entity compliance with HIPAA Privacy and Security Standards. These responsibilities will include risk management plan implementation, monitoring, policies interpretation, review and modifications as needed.

K. Security Rule. "Security Rule" shall mean the final rule adopting standards for the security of electronic protected health information as required by the Administrative Simplification title of the Health Insurance Portability and Accountability Act of 1996

(HIPAA) at 45 CFR Part 160 and Part 164, Subparts A and C as amended.

L. Workforce. "Workforce" shall mean every worker at Covered Entity without regard to their status. This includes physicians, residents, students, employees, contractors, business associates, consultants, temporaries, volunteers, interns, etc.

III. SECURITY MANAGEMENT PROCESS

All administrative safeguards requirements apply to business associates in the same way they apply to covered entities.

A. Assign Security Responsibility (R) 164.308(a)(2)

The Covered Entity will identify and assign privacy and security responsibilities to designated individual(s).

Procedure: *The Covered Entity leadership will identify individual(s) responsible for Privacy and Security safeguards and rule compliance. The privacy and security responsibilities can be assigned jointly to one individual or can be assigned to two individuals. The individual(s) position description(s) should be updated to reflect assigned duties and the template Security Official* ***Designation should be used to*** *document the designation. The HR manager will review and update the form, and assure document retention. Specific responsibilities of the Security Official shall include:*

a. *Ensuring privacy and security policies, procedures, and standards are in place and adhered to by entity;*
b. *Providing basic privacy and security support for all systems and users;*
c. *Providing on-going employee privacy and security education;*
d. *Performing periodic contingency plans, data classification and systems' audits/log review;*
e. *Managing system(s) users and overseeing information use;*
f. *Reviewing, approving, revoking and tracking requests for use of Personal Mobile Devices (PMD). Monitoring PMD use;*
g. *Reporting regularly to the Covered Entity Owner on entity's status with regard to HIPAA Privacy and Security compliance;*

B. Risk Analysis (R) 164.308(a)(1)(ii)(A)

A periodic comprehensive Risk Analysis of all Covered Entity assets including Information Systems will be conducted periodically. The risk analysis will be performed following industry best practice standards as described by HHS, NIST, ISACA, HIMSS or AHIMA organizations. The comprehensive Risk Analysis will be completed annually, and not less frequently than every two years, or after successful implementation of any major system change. Major system change would include: office relocation, replacement of EHR system containing PHI etc. Risk Analysis can be supplemented by documented components' risk assessment when reasonable and cost effective (e.g. hardware replacement).

Procedure: *The objective of the risk assessment procedure is to complete comprehensive, periodic and independent review of Covered Entity privacy and security vulnerabilities. The Covered Entity leadership will identify frequency and format of the risk assessment (self-risk assessment versus third party, independent risk assessment), and document it with the contract or project plan. The risk assessment process should include review of administrative, physical and technical safeguards, shall include assets criticality, threat frequency, impact analysis and creation of risk profile identifying mitigation strategies. The risk assessment shall include a comprehensive risk score and executive level summary report. Same concepts shall apply to third party risk assessments. Third party credentials shall be verified and should include ONC IT recommended CHPS, CPHIMS or CISA, CISM, CISSP with focus on healthcare.*

C. Risk Management (R)

The Security Official will be responsible for implementation of the Risk Management Plan. The Covered Entity Risk Management activities will include the following elements:

a. Development of the Risk Management Plan and Strategies based on the comprehensive Risk Analysis, the plan development can be completed in-house or it can be outsourced. The Risk Management Plan will include risks and mitigation strategies prioritization, and implementation plan for selected security measures.
b. Information system audit and evaluation will be conducted as scheduled in the monitoring schedule and monitoring report.
c. Implementation and evaluation of the Risk Management Plan will be coordinated by Covered Entity Security Official.

Procedure: *The objective of the risk management procedure is to document planned risk management approach.*

a. *The most recent risk assessment shall be used to develop or modify the risk management plan for the Covered Entity.*
b. *The plan shall include implementation specifics and timelines for selected risk mitigation strategies (security measures) identified in risk profile or risk assessment final report, and shall describe processes for regular organizational review of activity on its information systems containing ePHI.*
c. *Security Official will follow the monitoring schedule established in Covered Entity Risk Management Plan and will be responsible for implementation of the business and information system activity review per item E. Information System Activity Review of this policy.*

When selecting monitoring activities/reports focus on what is available through your monitoring systems or operating system (e.g. antivirus reports, patch or reliability reports). Complement monitoring with walk through audits, device and software inventory and user list reviews, SIEM if available.

D. **Sanction Policy (R)(disciplinary actions)**

To ensure the enforceability of the Covered Entity policies and procedures a Workforce Sanctions policy is established. Workforce violations of the Covered Entity policies and procedures will be documented and reviewed. Appropriate actions will be taken, against workforce who does not comply with organizational privacy and security policies and procedures. These actions range from verbal warning to contract/employment termination. Possible disciplinary action must be instituted for, but are not limited to the following policy violations:

a. Unauthorized disclosure of PHI or Confidential Information including information sharing through social media (e.g. Twitter, Facebook etc.), email, phone.
b. Unauthorized PHI or PII access (snooping);
c. Unauthorized disclosure of a User ID or password, attempting to obtain or using User ID or password that belongs to another person;
d. Unauthorized use of an authorized password to invade patient privacy by examining records or information for which there has been no request for review;
e. Installing or using software on computers without system manager or security official permission;
f. Installing or using unlicensed or pirated software on computers;

g. The intentional, unauthorized destruction of information;
h. Theft or attempted theft; negligent, unsafe performance of duty; failure to report on-the-job accidents or injuries, or safety hazards; absence without notification; insubordination;
i. Falsification of payroll or billing records; making false derogatory statements about company or coworkers; personal use of company property without authorization;

Procedure: *The objective of this Workforce Sanctions Policy procedure is to apply comparable discipline for comparable violations across the board regardless of the status of the violator.*

Structured format of applying workforce sanctions is important in improving: consistency of corrective actions, compliance, response promptness, strengthening trust and position for dispute resolution and improving Covered Entity position in case of lawsuits, civil actions, penalties and fines. Security Official will be responsible for implementation of the Workforce Sanctions Policy Procedure.

a. Upon discovery of the policy violation Security Official will notify Covered Entity leadership and will investigate and verify the violation. The Security Official shall use (as needed) SECURITY INCIDENT RESPONSE FORM to document the incident, findings and evidence. When SECURITY INCIDENT RESPONSE FORM is not used alternative fact-finding documentation shall be maintained.

b. Upon determination/confirmation of the policy violation the Security Official shall complete the SANCTION SEVERITY DETERMINATION FORM categorizing the violation, documenting factors increasing or decreasing sanctions severity and suggesting appropriate sanctions.

c. Final determination of the appropriate sanctions will be made with the Covered Entity leadership.

Sanctions shall be applied appropriately to employee performance issues like:

No call/no shows for work
Unexcused absence
Actions and behaviors jeopardizing health or safety of employees or consumers
Offensive or unethical behaviors
Significant fiscal or administrative errors
Fraud or theft in office

Following factors will guide Security Official in determining appropriate sanctions:

CATEGORY	EXPOSURE	NUMBER OF INDIVIDUALS AFFECTED	PURPOSE	SPECIAL PROTECTION	INTENT and PHI DISCLOSURE
1	Low external exposure to the organization	Involves a single patient	Carelessness, lack of education /training or poor judgment	No additional state or federal protection	Unintentional and unauthorized, PHI disclosure occurred
2	No external exposure to the organization	Involves 1 - 5 patients	Snooping or curiosity	Employees, VIP	Deliberate and unauthorized, no PHI disclosure
3	Medium external exposure to the organization	Involves 1 - 99 patients	Snooping or curiosity	Employees, VIP	Deliberate and unauthorized, PHI disclosure occurred
4	High external exposure to the organization	Involves 100+ patients	Malice, sale or personal gain	HIV, mental health, adoption, minor, substance abuse, genetic data	Deliberate and unauthorized, PHI disclosure occurred

*<u>FACTORS **INCREASING** SANCTION SEVERITY</u>*
Multiple offense
Harm incurred to victim(s)
High volume of victims or data
Breach of specially protected information
High exposure to organization
Hampered investigation
Large expense incurred (e.g. cost of breach)
Negative influence of actions on others

*<u>FACTORS **DECREASING** SANCTION SEVERITY</u>*
Occurred with good intentions (i.e., patient care, assist operations)
No harm to victim(s)
Volunteered /reported breach
Confessed/ cooperated with investigation
Showed remorse
Acted under direction of authority
Low cost to organization
Inadequate training

<u>Sanctions will include:</u>
Verbal warning (documented)
Written warning
Probation
Final warning w/suspension w/pay
Final warning w/suspension w/o pay
Demotion
Reduction in work hours
Loss of medical staff privileges
Contract severance
Employment termination

Sanction policies are closely related to employee performance evaluation, and any disciplinary actions shall be reflected in periodic performance evaluations.

D. Information System Activity Review (R)

The Covered Entity Risk Management Plan shall identify monitoring and auditing schedules for information systems including those containing electronic PHI (ePHI). Monitoring activities shall include periodic vulnerability testing, log review, walkthrough audits, access list review, port scanning and penetration testing. Security Official shall follow the monitoring schedule of activity review of information systems containing ePHI, and shall report to Covered Entity leadership periodically about policy violations, findings and sanctions.

Procedure: *This procedure describes processes for regular organizational review of activity on its information systems containing ePHI. Security Official will follow the monitoring schedule established in Covered Entity Risk Management Plan (see example below) and will be responsible for implementation of the Information System Activity Review Procedure.*

a. *The Security Official will run "individuals' access/permissions" report in XYZ system and download it to Excel. The workforce names on the report will be compared to listing of current workforce RM-2_WORKFORCE. This report will be run every 2 months.*
b. *The Security Official will complete the WALK_THROUGH audit every month.*
c. *The Firewall/access/end point security reports like TrendMicro WFBS-SVC report will be reviewed and saved every week. Identify other specific review steps for XYZ system(s) – firewall, prescription, EHR access reports TBD*
d. *The Security Official will complete the Privacy and Security RM_MONITORING CALENDAR/ dashboard/ REPORT and share it with Covered Entity leadership.*
e. *The Privacy and Security MONITORING – dashboard/ REPORT will be presented, reviewed and signed off by leadership monthly. Security Official will bring up issues between reporting periods as needed with leadership. All sanction, access termination decisions will be approved by Covered Entity leadership before implementing.*
f. *The log review documentation and all monitoring schedules and reports will be maintained in regularly backup soft copy in Risk Management folder. Annual soft CD copy will be maintained in Risk Management binder.*

Some wireless adapters come with utility software allowing for access logging. These can be utilized in light of lack of other access logging capabilities.

SECURITY AND PRIVACY MONITORING AND AUDITING SCHEDULE 20XX (Example)												
Month	Jan	Feb	Mar	Apr	May	June	July	Aug	Sept	Oct	Nov	Dec
XYZ System Access vs. payroll	X	X	X	X	X	X	X	X	X	X	X	X
Device inventory	X			X			X			X		
Vulnerability testing			X			X			X			X
Wireless Access			X			X			X			X
HIPAA Walk-through Audits	X	X	X	X	X	X	X	X	X	X	X	X

PRIVACY AND SECURITY MONITORING - REPORT (Example)		TIME PERIOD:	January 1st – March 31st
AUDITS PERFORMED	**SCOPE**	**FINDINGS**	**FOLLOW-UP /DATE**
Wireless Access	*Verified network is PSWD protected Reviewed firewall report for March*	*Wireless connection secured*	*None indicated*
Staff Access to ePHI in XYZ System	*Computer system access compared to payroll*	*5 individuals with access are not on payroll. Appropriate access—3 Access removed for 2 users.*	*Re-check in 6 months. Need to remove user's access immediately after they are terminated from the organization.*
Walk through	*Facility walkthrough*	*Visitors sign in not enforced*	*Remind all staff about visitors sign in requirement*
Security Issues Vulnerability scans	*Scan Computer system*	*3 systems show outdated software and high level vulnerabilities*	*Implement updates, address vulnerabilities Re-scan in 6 months.*
Total Sanctions:	Verbal Warning:		
	Written Warning:		
	Terminations:		

IV. WORKFORCE SECURITY and INFORMATION ACCESS MANAGEMENT

The purpose of the policies and procedures of this section is to ensure that all members of the Covered Entity workforce have appropriate access to ePHI, access is authorized, supervised, modified and properly terminated as needed.

A. <u>Personal Mobile Devices</u>

The Covered Entity Workforce will NOT use unauthorized Personal Mobile Devices (laptops, smartphones, external drives etc.) to store, access, send or process ePHI or Confidential Data under any circumstances. Specifically the use of Personal Mobile Devices to photograph, video or voice record ePHI and Confidential Data is prohibited.

The use of Personal Mobile Devices with Covered Entity systems and data may be permitted by Security Official under specific circumstances described below.

Procedure: *Individual can request permission for the Personal Mobile Device PMD use for work purposes. The individual has to complete the Personal Mobile Device Use Agreement (Attachment C) and submit it to the Security Official for review. This agreement will govern the use of such devices when the request is approved. The agreement will address specific administrative and technical requirements, end user obligations and employer rights.*

a. *The agreement has to be signed/approved before devices can be connected to or access Covered Entity systems.*
b. *Security Official will review the request and inspect the device (as needed) within 2 weeks.*
c. *Security Official will keep track of the PMDs permitted to access entity systems and can revoke such permissions at any time.*
d. *In case Personal Mobile Devices are permitted to be used with Covered Entity systems and data, all General Operations and Information Security Policies and Procedures will apply to these devices.*

B. **Use of PHI data**

The minimum necessary standard is not intended to impede the provision of quality health care. When using, communicating, transferring or printing the PHI, users must exercise sound judgment and include only the minimum necessary amount of information needed to fulfill the transaction or information request. User must use Designated Record Set and Legal Health Record documents to identify proper documentation for disclosure.

Procedure: *When faced with request for disclosure of PHI or PII read the request diligently, ask questions as needed to clarify what the requestor is asking for. Professional judgment will help determine the amount of information to be released.*

a. *Verify if the authorization to disclose information is necessary, look at the type of information requested, look for the disclosure purpose (TPO, school immunization, insurance underwriting, public health) and disclosure exception e.g. security exceptions, law enforcement etc. described in more detail under the privacy policies of this document.*

b. *Verify whether the authorization to disclose information is necessary and/or available. Disclosures of PHI pursuant to an authorization are exempt from the minimum necessary rule.*

c. *Use Designated Record Set chart to identify information/documents to be disclosed.*

d. *PHI that is used for educational or analytical purposes where possible shall be de-identified before use. De-identify data as needed.*

e. *Check the Privacy Rule Safeguards when dealing with use of PHI in emergency situations or when responding to patient's or law enforcement requests.*

f. *Suspicious behaviors among co-workers, volunteers or patients e.g. employees taking papers home, copying records when not part of job duties shall be reported immediately to Security Official.*

C. **Patient authentication**

This policy is to prevent unauthorized disclosure/access to PHI. Upon arrival, patient identity shall always be verified with government issued photo ID or with the picture taken during first visit and stored in the Electronic Health Record system. False identification used for obtaining services (e.g. false identity used for obtaining maternity care, but accurate info provided for birth certificate records) shall be reported immediately to Security Official as it may lead to, or may be the result of medical identity theft and fraud.

Before disclosing any PHI or Confidential Information over the phone, a positive identity validation needs to be completed. Staff needs to ask for two additional pieces of information (in addition to first and last name) and needs to validate them with the information contained in practice EHR/PM system.

Procedure*: Use* ***E****xplain,* ***V****erify,* ***A****sk* ***(EVA)*** *Patient Authentication PROCEDURE.*

During the first patient encounter the receptionist shall make a digital copy of government issued ID and store it in the Electronic Health Records system (if possible), verify patient identity and take patient's digital picture to be stored in the Electronic Health Record System (when system functionality allows) for verification during subsequent visits. The picture stored in the EHR shall be updated every 7 years or when significant appearance changes occur.

When responding to patients' phone call and request for health information, the Covered Entity staff shall always authenticate the caller before providing health information over the phone e.g. lab results, doctors diagnosis or when scheduling specific procedures. While staff (especially in smaller practice) may be familiar with patient's voice and authentication questions may seem redundant, the questions will communicate the practice attention to privacy and security of patients' records and will reinforce patient's trust, the patients will appreciate that. In addition to patient's first and last name, combination of any of the following two elements must be used for positive identification:

- *Last five/four digits of SSN*
- *Date of birth*
- *Patients' address*
- *Insurance card number*
- *Telephone number*

*The **E**xplain, **V**erify, **A**sk (**EVA**) shall be used in training and shall be readily available to staff responding to patient's inquiries as e.g. a cue card printed and posted by the telephone:*

a. ***Explain** - that authentication or verification of patient's identity is important for patients to protect them from medical identity theft and to maintain privacy of their health information.*
b. ***Verify** - patient's first, last name and their date of birth with what is in your system/file. Use: Mr. IdentityThieve what is your birth date? Instead of: Is your birth date January 1st 1970?*
c. ***Ask** - for additional information you already have in your system/file, so you can verify it with what the caller tells you: "Mr. IdentityThieve, for verification purposes could you please tell me what the last four digits of your social security number (insurance card) are?" Or "What are your address and the phone number I can reach you at? Do you have a cell phone number?" Instead of: "Are you still at 2525 IKnowWhereYouLive Street? Is your phone still 614-444-4444?*

D. **Email, text, web, social media and oral communications and use**

This policy is to prevent inappropriate use, unauthorized disclosure/access to PHI.

Procedure:
Workforce shall always be aware of their surroundings when discussing PHI and Confidential Information or communicating through email, text or social media to avoid shoulder browsing.

a. ***Oral (phone) communications***
Workforce shall not discuss PHI or Confidential Information in public areas if the information can be overheard. This includes the use of cellular telephones in public areas. Caution

shall be used when conducting conversations in: semi-private rooms, waiting rooms, corridors, elevators, stairwells, cafeterias, restaurants, or on public transportation.

b. ***Email***

Email is a versatile communication tool often used for spam and phishing, which aids hackers in obtaining your password to e.g. banking sites or allows them to download malware or spyware to your computer, to steal information (e.g. passwords) or gain control of your computer and use it for illegal or malicious purposes or deny access to your computer.

- *Email system shall not be used for creation or transmission of offensive or disruptive messages including offensive comments about disabilities, religion, race, sex, political campaigns etc., distribution of chain letters or pornography. Employees receiving any emails with such content shall immediately notify Security Official.*
- *Company email shall not be used for personal matters. All email communications stored on or conducted with company devices belong to the company and can be requested, viewed and/or monitored by company managers.*
- *All email and text communications containing ePHI or confidential information must be secure/encrypted, emails that do not contain ePHI do not have to be encrypted.*
- *Senders must use disclaimer in their emails e.g.: "This message contains information that may be confidential or privileged. The information is intended solely for the recipient and its use by any other party is not authorized. If you are not the intended recipient, be aware that any disclosure, copying, distribution or use of the contents of this information is prohibited. Please notify the sender if you received this email in error and delete the original."*
- *Senders shall pay special attention when completing address line of an email, and making sure the electronic communications are addressed to intended individuals. It is best to directly respond to email from individuals or to copy the email address instead of typing it to avoid misdirected emails.*
- *Exercise caution when responding to unsolicited email; do not provide personal or confidential information (e.g. account numbers, SSN).*
- *Exercise caution when opening email attachments. Your computer will recognize most of the file attachments and will identify software to open them like MS Word or Adobe for PDF files.*

- *Files with .exe extension or those not recognized shall be treated with caution, do not open/click on files with .exe extensions and consult with security official when in doubt about other files. Exercise caution when clicking on links within email. Copy and paste links into web browser address bar is a good practice.*
- *Use company email only for business related subscriptions (newsletters, blogs etc.).*
- *Authenticate email senders by checking digital signature (when used) or calling them.*
- *Texting PHI is not permitted unless secure messaging solution is identified and approved by Security Official. Texting while driving is prohibited.*

c. ***Web/internet usage***
While using web interface to submit ePHI, demographic or confidential information (e.g. filling out forms) make sure the connection is secure.

- *When login is necessary make sure you verify the web address before entering user and password data. The secure connection is indicated by https and padlock in web browser address bar. Newest technology also identifies the secure connection by making the address bar green and identifying the company name. You can hoover your mouse over the company name or click it to see the authentication details.*
- *Make sure you are using approved and updated web browser, and be mindful that sometimes websites may not be available due to external factors e.g. web server failure, hackers attack on the website, network interruptions etc.*
- *Never allow the web browser or web application to remember, store your login credentials: user ID and password.*
- *In general internet use on company networks and devices, unrelated to company business is not permitted. Visiting immoral, offensive and illegal websites, downloading unapproved or illegal software is prohibited and will result in disciplinary actions.*

d. ***Social Media***
Workforce shall pay special attention to privacy and personally identifiable information when using social media. Use of clusters of descriptors (procedure, gender, facility, time, even without name, SSN, DOB) can still create identifiable information. Sharing patient's photos without their written permission is a violation of Privacy Rule.

- *Employees shall not use company emails for personal social media accounts (e.g. Facebook, Instagram, Twitter).*
- *Employees should be mindful about organization reputation when making statements about the organization when interacting through social media.*
- *Employees shall exercise caution when their own social media interactions, name and activities can be associated with the organization.*
- *When employee notices issues arising from social media, employee should bring it immediately to the attention of (Title/Function/Name) or security official.*
- *The harassment or discrimination related issues taking place through social media and outside of the work place space, but work related, should also be brought up immediately to organization attention.*
- *The (Title/Function/Name) will coordinate responses to issues arising from social media communications with security official.*
- *Only designated practice representative (Title/ Function/Name) can communicate about company through social media like Facebook, Twitter, LinkedIn etc. and will monitor social media attitude towards the organization.*
- *The social media/web communications forms may include: discussion postings, press releases', interviews (identify other forms specific to the organization). These communications need to be coordinated/approved by designated individual.*
- *The communication topics should be limited to: organization news releases, promotions, hiring's, event and event participation announcements.*
- *Company related social media activities outside of working hours will not count towards employees' time payable unless specifically approved prior to those activities taking place.*

E. **Access Authorization and/or Supervision (A)**

Access to organization information systems will be authorized and supervised by Security Official.

Procedure:

Authorization to access organization computers, ePHI and/or systems containing ePHI will be granted/approved by Security Official in consultation with organization leadership/HR, upon workforce employment or engagement starting date. Access will be granted on the "need to know" basis, and role-based access shall be used when permitted by system. Following guidance for access authorization will be used:

a. *Access to Electronic Health Records system shall be limited to staff performing clinical functions e.g. physicians, nurses.*
b. *Prescription approval or printing will be authorized only for eligible staff;*
c. *Access to Practice Management systems containing ePHI shall be limited to workforce performing respective function e.g. billing, scheduling and record management staff.*
d. *Security Official will complete periodic Information System(s) Activity Review, identify access appropriateness and take corrective actions as needed. Access modifications will be handled by Security Official in consultation with organization IT, HR and leadership.*

F. **Workforce clearance policy (A)** Before employment and before granting access to Covered Entity systems and ePHI, the workforce background will be verified through employment history, education, BMV, Background check, or business status verification.

Procedure:

The Covered Entity workforce clearance policies objective is to safeguard business assets, reputation, PHI and Confidential Information. The clearance shall be completed before engaging in business relationship (employment or contractual relationship). Workforce clearance procedures will be handled as follows:

a. *The Covered Entity Security Official (or designated person) will verify and maintain workforce information including: name, address, contact information, access to ePHI systems, access authorization, background check, HIPAA training, equipment assignments etc. in eRM-2_WORKFORCE document. At least two elements of workforce credentials shall be verified:*

- *Licensure, education, certification, training – through official transcript, web resource e.g. HIMSS, AHIMA lists of certified individuals or* ***National Practitioner Data Bank*** *(NPDB) http://www.npdb-hipdb.hrsa.gov.*
- *Past employment history – through calling, verifying at least two references.*
- *Background check – through BMV record check or Bureau of Criminal Investigations (BCI), Criminal Offender Record Information. State Attorney General Office usually provides list of providers for background check. In Ohio visit http://www.ohioattorneygeneral.gov*
- *Other sources of background check (specific to some jobs) may include: Sex Offender Registry, Nurse Aide (Assistant) Registry, Department of Developmental Disabilities abuse registry...*
- *Business status of independent contractors and business associates – verify business through Secretary of State (SOS) Business Name Search. Some States, like for example*

Ohio provide the Certificate of Good Standing which can be requested from any business you are contracting with, you shall follow SOS instructions and verify the Certificate Validation number. For high dollar amount and long term business engagements in Ohio you may elect to sign up for Email Filling Notification about your contractor/business associate under Business Information/Filling Notification section. This notification will let you know if for example business is being dissolved. Ohio also provides a list of Debarred Contractors under Business Services/Record section of the Secretary Of State website, the list is not long and provides additional insight.

b. *HR manager, owner will make the final hiring and termination decisions for all employees and contractors*

G. **Termination policy (A)**

Access authorization to ePHI will be terminated by Security Official immediately after end of engagement/employment.

Procedure:

a. *Security Official will terminate access to ePHI immediately after workforce termination or end of contractor's engagement no later than 1 day after termination. Upon employment termination HR will send an email to Security Official, indicating termination date. Security official will terminate employee access to system(s) and document the access termination by completing the Staff Separation Checklist and forwarding it to HR. When possible an advanced notice of employee/contractor termination shall be sent.*
b. *Terminating user access may be accomplished through user account deletion. When user account deletion is not feasible, the Security Official shall "lock" the account with new, unique password. The transaction capabilities for the account shall be disabled.*
c. *When access to terminated employee account and documents is needed, security official will assign and maintain new, unique password to that account.*
d. *Security official will conduct periodic review of inactive or "locked" accounts (every 6 months) to determine feasibility of account deletion*
e. *Equipment and devices assigned to an individual shall be accounted for and collected before employee termination.*
f. *The access can also be terminated as directed by organization leadership or as determined through the Information System(s) Activity Review. The decision to terminate access shall be documented.*

H. Isolating Health Care Clearinghouse Functions (A). Not applicable to small/medium practices.

I. **Access Establishment and Modification (A)**

Access will be authorized, established and modified by Security Official.

Procedure: *Access modifications will be handled by Security Official in consultation with organization IT, HR and leadership. All access changes (e.g. ePHI access establishment or termination) shall be documented in RM-2_WORKFORCE document.*

a. Security Official (in collaboration with HR and IT system manager) will coordinate unique user IDs assignment and system access, to all workforce members to facilitate users' identification and authenticate access to various information systems especially those containing ePHI.
b. Security Official will communicate all authorizations and modifications in writing to appropriate staff.
c. Use of shared User IDs shall be prohibited unless specific functional needs warrant exceptions from this rule. The Security Official will review and approve shared credentials use on case-by-case basis. The exception needs to be documented and managed.
d. Remote Access to organization network and information systems from outside will be limited, access will be granted by Security Official on a case-by-case basis, per individual user or application. PHI and Confidential Information that is stored or accessed remotely must maintain the same level of protections as information stored and accessed within the organization network. Thus strong authentication (including two-factor authentication) may be required as determined by the Security Official. Please also see Personal Mobile Devices (PMD) section of this policy when remote access is requested for PMDs.
e. Computers running systems containing PHI shall be used only for job/health related purposes.

V. SECURITY AWARENESS AND TRAINING

The purpose of this policy is to maintain, document and improve workforce use of security related best practices to safeguard organization information and information systems.

A. **Security Reminders (A)** The Covered Entity workforce will be provided with quarterly reminders/updates highlighting information security best practices including protection from malicious software, log-in and password management. Covered Entity shall provide (or require completion of) annual

HIPAA Privacy and Security refresher trainings. The completion of the training shall be documented in eRM-2_WORKFORCE document.

Procedure: *Security Official will provide quarterly reminders/updates highlighting information privacy security best practices including protection from malicious software, log-in and password management.*

a. *Security Official will distribute emails (newsletter) and bulletin board postings, and the workforce members are required to read and implement best practices. The reminders shall also include examples of common privacy and security pitfalls leading to data breaches, federal investigations and/or penalties.*
b. *Security Official will distribute quizzes testing staff privacy and security awareness. Quiz results shall be reviewed and documented to improve training.*
c. *Security Official will utilize training materials available at e.g.: http://www.healthit.gov/providers-professionals/ehr-privacy-security*
d. *Security Official will arrange for annual HIPAA privacy and security awareness training. The completion of the training shall be documented in RM-2_WORKFORCE document, or in the form of retained attendance list or certificate of training completion. Documented two Continuing Education (CE) credits obtained for related training can substitute annual refresher training.*

B. **Protection from Malicious Software (A)** The Covered Entity shall implement tools to protect organizations systems from malware, and shall educate its workforce on the proper use of these tools.

Procedure:

a. *Security Official shall ensure that anti-virus, anti-spyware software licenses are renewed, and the automatic updates for these applications are turned on. Periodic system review shall be used to document the review.*
b. *Users shall never turn off or disable virus checking or anti-spyware software approved and installed on their computers.*
c. *Users shall observe anti-virus and anti-spyware software warnings when visiting website or downloading attachments. User shall not enter websites or download content when they are warned about it by antivirus or anti malware software or when they have any suspicions.*

d. *Occasionally the anti-virus or anti-malware software may stop working. This may result from e.g. Denial of Service attack. The software should be immediately turned on and user should notify Security Official about the incident immediately.*
e. *Users shall never install unauthorized software on organization computers. Users shall always seek approval before installing software.*
f. *Users shall never open files with file extensions that are likely to be associated with malware (e.g., .bat, .com, .exe, .pif, .vbs);*
g. *User shall never open suspicious emails or email attachments, clicking on hyperlinks, etc. from unknown or known senders, or visiting websites that are likely to contain malicious content or clicking on suspicious web browser popup windows;*
h. *In case malicious software is detected or suspected, users shall immediately inform Security Official who will seek resolution (e.g. with IT partner).*

C. **Log-in Monitoring (A) and Password Management (A)**
The Covered Entity shall implement tools to secure and monitor user's log-in to company systems, and shall communicate and enforce password management best practices.
Procedures:
a. *Passwords must not be written and easily accessible around the workstation.*
b. *Passwords must never be shared with another individual. Users will be held accountable for all actions performed on the system with their User ID (log-in monitoring).*
c. *Default Passwords provided with devices have to be changed upon installation and password reset disk will be created and maintained by Security Official (if applicable). While other password reset options may be used (depending on network settings), clear access controls need to be maintained in form of user lists including users with administrative privileges.*
d. *Information systems shall be setup to* ***enforce strong passwords (minimum 12 characters), enforce password complexity, history, requirement for frequent changes (e.g. 90 days), user lockout and time out when password entered incorrectly*** *5 times. Use CIS standards as guidance in security policies setting.*
e. *When possible consider using passphrase (longer form of password), which can be a combination of*

two or more words. For example: "Three-creeks" or "3-CreeKS"

f. *PASSWORD requirements:*

- *Use a combination of uppercase and lowercase letters, as well as numbers, spaces, and/or symbols. Password complexity means using characters from three of the following four categories: Lower case: a-z, Upper case: A – Z, Base 10 digits: 0 – 9, Non alphabetical characters e.g.: !, $, &, +;*
- *Use strong passwords at least 8 characters long, the longer the password, the stronger the password. It takes significantly more time to crack a 12 character password than a 6 character password. Avoid predictable patterns, such as the alphabet, family names or addresses, common phrases, lyrics, or quotations;*
- *Use different usernames and passwords for different websites and systems you access;*
- *Consider using a password vault to securely store various passwords e.g. lastpass.com (see item (i));*
- *For websites that you visit infrequently, consider generating random passwords made up of nonsensical characters. When you lose or forget your password you can always reset it.*
- *Change your passwords every 90 days.*

g. *Log-in to systems containing ePHI access will be monitored by Security Official by following monitoring schedule and reviewing user lists and access logs.*

h. *The use of computers with biometric readers shall be promoted to enhance security and ease user's access and authentication.*

i. *When using biometric readers Security Official will make sure that readers are adjusted to implement high reader sensitivity to assure high level of authentication (low false acceptance rate), and that password vaults are storing passwords in encrypted format.*

j. *Use multifactor authentication (MFA) for especially remote access, access to cloud resources and access for admins.*

VI. SECURITY POLICIES AND PROCEDURES

The purpose of these policies and procedures is to establish controls and processes for responding to unexpected incidents and emergency situations that may affect PHI, mitigate their harmful effects, protect Covered Entity PHI and ensure business recovery.

A. **Security Incident Response and Reporting (R).** The purpose of this policy is to identify and respond to suspected or known security incidents; mitigate, to the extent practicable, harmful effects of security incidents that are known to the covered entity; and document security incidents and their outcomes. All workforce members are required to promptly report suspected or known security incidents to Security Official. Examples of security incidents include: data/equipment theft or loss, unauthorized access or use, inadvertent email distribution, policy violation, virus, malware or spyware infection, hacking incident, inappropriate use of media/social media.

Data breach is generally, an impermissible use or disclosure under the Privacy Rule that compromises the security or privacy of the protected health information, **unless covered entity or business associate can demonstrate that there is a low probability that the protected health information has been compromised**, or one of the exceptions to the data breach definition applies. Part 164 Section §164.402 - §164.410 address data breach and notification requirements.

Breach definition includes following exceptions:

- Unintentional acquisition, access or use by employee (acting under authority),
- Accidental disclosure between authorized employees,
- When there is a good faith believe that information could not have been retained by unauthorized individual, to whom impermissible disclosure was made.

While the above definition of PHI data breach comes from the HIPAA Omnibus rule, the same concepts can be applied to personally identifiable information (PII).

Massachusetts defines the data breach as unauthorized acquisition or use of unencrypted personal information (can be PHI or PII data), that creates substantial risk of identity theft or fraud for the individual. Other States' data breach definitions are similar (201 CMR 17.00 Standards for the protection of personal information of residents of the Commonwealth).

Procedure:

This procedure describes event triggers and steps to be taken in case of security incident. Security Official will be responsible for implementation of this Security Incident Response Procedure.

a. The most serious security incidents are those resulting in data breach (see definition above). Use eSECURIY_ INCIDENT_RESPONSE.xlsx DECISION CHART to investigate and document, factors to consider in assessing the probability of PHI being compromised include:

- *What type of data has been compromised, what are the data elements involved and how likely data can be re-identified;*
- *Who is the unauthorized person who used the protected health information or to whom the disclosure was made;*
- *Was the protected health information actually acquired or viewed only; and*
- *The extent to which the risk to the protected health information has been mitigated (what were the immediate mitigation steps).*

Security incident risk assessment, considering the above factors will help identify the high or low probability of data being compromised, and will determine need for data breach notification. It is necessary to ***retain the copy of the security incident report and risk assessment*** *in all situations, even when level of information compromise is low and no breach notification is necessary.*

b. *Section §164.402 - §164.410 address data breach and notification requirements and additional information is provided in SECURITY INCIDENT RESPONSE form.*
   - *Indicators of possible security incident: unfamiliar individuals are within restricted or secure areas of the organization e.g. records room, server room; break in e.g. broken window or locks; theft/loss of electronic devices (e.g. PC, copier, backup drive) in office; theft/loss of health paper records in office; loss of portable devices possibly containing PHI e.g. phone, tablet, flash drive, back up device or media like CD/DVD; email containing PHI sent to wrong recipient, paper documents containing PHI sent to wrong recipient; unauthorized PHI access e.g. snooping, looking up coworker, neighbor or VIP records; sharing PHI with or through media, friends; noticing content, software or applications (malware) not permitted or approved for use; noticing erratic equipment behavior e.g. PC/software performing unfamiliar tasks, PC rebooting multiple times without user action. Policy violations like password sharing are also considered security incidents. Security Incidents can also be uncovered through review of audit logs, patient's complaints, business associates notifications and media.*

c. *Security Official shall be notified immediately when security incident is suspected. Upon notification the Security Official shall:*
   - *Immediately investigate the issue and complete the SECURITY INCIDENT RESPONSE form to evaluate the*

situation and document the investigation. The form contains additional guidance and information about data breaches.

- *Record all security incidents in the eSECURITY_INCIDENT RESPONSE.xlsx document, and determine if completion of SECURITY_INCIDENT_REPORT is necessary.*
- *When incidents involve equipment (e.g. PC, laptop, storage device), the Security Official needs to take immediate ownership of the equipment suspected in security incident to facilitate its inspection and completion of the investigation. The equipment, including personally owned devices needs to be secured and not accessible to others to avoid possibilities of tampering with evidence. As needed the specialized data forensic services may need to be employed.*
- *In case of a* ***computer theft****, which employed cloud back up services, please follow backup service provider steps and suggestions. These steps may include call for* ***immediate data restoration****, geo-location of the lost computer to aid police in computer retrieval and account cancelation – see Data Backup Procedure as well.*
- *Notify organization leadership upon confirmation of incident or when suspected incident may result in data breach.*
- *Organization leadership with Security Official shall determine additional steps to verify potential for data breach and need for breach notification. The* ***investigation steps*** *will be unique to each situation but may include: interviews with workforce, review of EHR system audit trail reports, forensic review of computers and records, inventory review, staff and patients attendance (time cards/sign in sheets), review of janitorial/maintenance schedules etc.* ***Isolating affected equipment*** *for computer forensics shall also be considered especially in case of suspected data breach.*
- *Data breaches by Business Associates are quite common. Proper Business Associate (BA) agreement is a key in mitigating the Covered Entity risk exposure. In case of the data breach caused by BA, a review of BA contract, their records and establishing good communications and collaboration in the investigation process is essential.*
- *If it is clear that the security incident* ***does not*** *result in data breach, sanction policy and other corrective actions may still have to be applied. The workforce Sanction Policy shall be used to determine sanction steps.*
- *If it is clear that the security incident* ***likely resulted*** *in data breach the SECURITY INCIDENT RESPONSE form should help identify actions necessary to mitigate data*

breach results, actions necessary to comply with HIPAA rules, and individuals to be included in addressing the incident. Organization/Covered Entity shall consider at least including Legal Counsel and Privacy and Security expert in developing plan to address data breach.

d. ***Before issuing any data breach notification*** *and following HHS Breach Notification rule described at http://www.hhs.gov/ocr/privacy/hipaa/administrative/breachnotificationrule/index.html the Covered Entity leadership and Security Official shall conduct thorough investigation verifying that data breach in fact occurred, and account for number of individuals affected by data breach, as reporting responsibilities differ based on number of individuals affected (500+).* ***Ask for second opinion.***

B. **Contingency Plan – Data Backup Plan (R)** The data backup plan must assure availability of retrievable exact copies of critical information created and maintained by organization (including PHI). Backup plan must be documented and routinely updated; backup data must be stored off-site for a specific period of time, must be protected from physical damage, and must be afforded the same level of protection as the original data.

Procedure:
There are two procedures to backup organization data. Security Official will be responsible for implementation of the Data Backup Procedure.

a. *Following computers and respective files will be covered by the backup plan: [List files/PCs]*
b. *The automatic online data backup with [Vendor name] is scheduled and maintained on the computer(s) containing PHI data. This service provides constant back-up capabilities in a secure, encrypted format. In case of internet connectivity interruptions, the alternative backup procedure (below) will maintain data integrity and availability.*
c. *When on line backup is setup, turning on the geo-location/mapping services may be helpful in case of a computer theft. Mapping may help police to locate/recover the stolen computer when it is connected to the internet.*
d. *Follow backup service provider data recovery steps and suggestions, which may include:*
   - *Immediate data recovery;*
   - *Filing police reports and sharing geo-location/mapping details;*
   - *Closing of the backup account after data is recovered and location is established.*

e. *The daily automatic backup procedure will be scheduled and maintained on the computer(s) (ENTER PC NAME) containing PHI data. The data will be backup on the network PC (NAS or password protected external drive in encrypted format) at 5 PM. After backup is completed the Security Official will disconnect the drive and store it off-site in fireproof safe.*

f. *The installable copy of the EHR software will be stored on DVD/hard drive in off-site location.*

C. **Contingency Plan – Disaster Recovery Plan (R)** The disaster recovery plan containing processes enabling the entity to restore any loss of data in the event of fire, theft, vandalism, natural disaster, or system failure must be developed and documented. The copy of this plan, along with the contact list has to be retained outside of the primary business location, so it is available in case of disaster affecting primary business location.

Procedure:

The following disaster recovery procedures will be used in case of disaster or incident destroying PHI. Security Official will be responsible for implementation of the Disaster Recovery (DR) Procedure. The copy of this plan, along with the contact list (call tree) has to be retained outside of the primary business location, so it is available to each response team member in case of disaster affecting primary business location. Following staff members will constitute DR team: [list staff names]

DR scenarios need to be developed for disasters most likely affecting the organization. Common scenarios shall include: extended power outage, water break, network and system outage, workplace violence, security incident, fire or natural disaster affecting the building.

eDRP_CONTINGENCY_PLAN form will help develop scenarios.

Understanding criticality of systems in case of disaster recovery is very important to prioritize recovery efforts. Larger organizations shall establish Recovery Time Objectives (RTO) (how quickly specific systems need to be returned to operational status) and Recovery Point Objectives (RPO) (how much data loss is acceptable in case of a disaster).

Some small/simple organizations may document the DRP as follows:

a. *In case of equipment e.g. hard drive failure the Security Official will:*
   - *Identify replacement PC or order equipment repair, and contact IT expert as needed.*

- *Install EHR software on repaired or replacement PC, assure passwords, encryption and other workstation security measures are functional.*
- *Recover ePHI from on line storage following vendor data recovery procedures.*

b. *In case of disaster destroying computer equipment at the office location (fire, water damage, tornado):*

- *In certain situations, when disaster situation occurs during work hours, when there is advanced notice, when building evacuation is imminent (time permitting and considering* ***people's safety first****), the Security Official may order all PCs to be powered off, all laptops currently used to be removed from the building during evacuation by staff using them. SO may remove/secure office backup drive when only small local backup is used. In disaster situation keep in mind that* ***people safety is a first priority****.*
- *Security Official will use backup PC stored at … (or acquire replacement PC), install EHR software, assure passwords, encryption and other workstation security measures are functional, and communicate the recovery location to leadership,*
- *Recover ePHI from on line storage following vendor data recovery procedures.*
- *In case the Internet access is not available the data will be recovered from secondary backup source, the encrypted backup drive.*

After internet access is restored, Security Official shall compare data from on line back up to data from local back up device and resolve any data issues. The size of the backup file, count of specific records can be used for comparison purposes.

D. **Contingency Plan - Emergency Mode Operation Plan (R) (Business Continuity Plan)** The emergency mode operation plan documents multiple emergency mode operations scenarios, documenting processes enabling the entity to continue to operate in the event of fire, vandalism, natural disaster, or system failure.

Procedure:

Following emergency mode operations scenarios will be used in case of emergency. Security Official will be responsible for implementation of the Emergency Mode Operations Procedure.

a. *In case of Electronic Health Records (EHR) system failure, power outage, vandalism:*

- *Security Official must be notified immediately.*
- *Security Official will evaluate the situation and determine if continuing operations is feasible. Staff shall print daily schedules one day in advance. Depending on system*

failure severity, staff may need to call and cancel daily appointments.

- *The organization may still be able to operate depending on paper charts availability. Front desk staff will use notebooks to collect patients contact information to schedule follow up visits after systems are restored. Billing and customer invoicing may have to be postponed after Practice Management or billing systems are restored as well.*

b. *In case of Fire or natural disaster destroying office and information systems:*

- *Security Official must be notified immediately. Security Official will contact organization leadership and determine action steps.*
- *The organization may not be able to operate, but may be required to provide emergency assistance to disaster victims or may be asked for assistance with victims' identification through medical records. To enable the emergency assistance with use of organization medical records, the appropriate disaster recovery scenario (fire, equipment destruction) will be implemented.*

In emergency situation Security Official must authorize access to organization information system(s) and ePHI, to individuals who previously were not authorized to access ePHI. Access for these individuals shall be promptly terminated after the emergency situation ends, and access authorization and termination shall be recorded as soon as possible in RM-2_WORKFORCE document.

E. **Contingency Plan-Testing and Revision Procedures (A)** Procedures shall be developed and documented requiring periodic testing of written contingency plans to discover weaknesses and the subsequent process of revising the documentation, if necessary.

Procedure:

The contingency plan testing will be conducted at least once a year. Following scenarios will be tested. Security Official will be responsible for implementation of the Testing Procedure.

a. *System failure will be simulated, the front desk system(s)/PCs will be shut down and will not be available. Front desk staff will admit patients without system availability, staff will use alternative tools and processes to capture patient's contact information and schedule future visits. The process/workflow review of providing care/services without EHR/systems availability will be conducted.*

b. *Equipment failure resulting in loss of PHI data will be simulated. Replacement equipment will be identified and Security Official will follow disaster recovery procedure reinstalling EHR software and restoring data following online procedures for data recovery.*

c. *Loss of office and data due to natural disaster in the area will be reviewed. The Security Official will conduct a process/workflow review of responding to this scenario: identifying alternative location, equipment, reinstalling systems/software and restoring data from encrypted hard drive.*

F. **Contingency Plan - Applications and Data Criticality Analysis (A)** The criticality of specific applications and data in support of other contingency plan components must be assessed and documented.

Procedure:

Criticality of the applications, systems and data will be assessed and documented during the risk analysis process.

a. *Security Official will be responsible for updating the RA3-ASSETS document when new critical assets are added.*
b. *Security Official will be responsible for amending contingency plans, inventory documents and action plans to reflect new assets or asset criticality changes.*

G. **Evaluation (R)** Organization/Covered Entity information systems periodic technical and non-technical evaluations, including evaluation of contingency plans will be performed in response to environmental or operational changes affecting the security of electronic PHI or PII to ensure its continued protection.

Procedure:

The evaluation of information systems is part of the Covered Entity Risk Management Plan and will be conducted as described in Section III E. Information System Activity Review.

Vulnerability testing, port scanning and penetration testing shall be scheduled periodically as warranted by the size of the organization. Automated monitoring systems shall be used to simplify monitoring and system evaluation.

The comprehensive evaluation of organization/Covered Entity systems will be conducted annually during completion of the Risk Analysis and development of the Risk Management Plan.

H. **Business Associate Contracts and Other Arrangements (R)** Covered Entity will incorporate written business associate agreements with all contractors and individuals creating, receiving, maintaining or transmitting PHI for or on behalf of Covered Entity, to safeguard protected and confidential information. Covered entity does not need to enter into business associate agreements with subcontractors of their business associate - business associates need to do so.

While provisions of the HIPAA Privacy and Security rule apply to business associates and their subcontractors, it might be a prudent business practice for high cost/high risk contracts to verify business associates (and vendors in non-business associates status) with some additional diligence described in procedure.

Procedure:

The following procedure will be used to determine the need and establish business associate contracts. Security Official will be responsible for implementation of the Business Associate Contract Procedure.

a. *Business associates are directly liable under the HIPAA Rules:*
   - *For impermissible uses and disclosures;*
   - *For a failure to provide breach notification to the covered entity;*
   - *For a failure to provide access to a copy of electronic protected health information to either the covered entity, the individual, or the individual's designee (whichever is specified in the business associate agreement);*
   - *For a failure to disclose protected health information where required by the Secretary to investigate or determine the business associate's compliance with the HIPAA Rules;*
   - *For a failure to provide an accounting of disclosures;*
   - *For a failure to comply with the requirements of the Security Rule;*
   - *For applying minimum necessary standard when disclosing PHI;*
   - *For assuring that their subcontractors comply with the same restrictions and condition;*
   - *For reporting breaches of unsecured PHI to covered entity;*
   - *For civil monetary penalties;*
   - *In general business associates are not required to designate privacy official or provide notice of privacy practices unless such responsibility is delegated to business associate as a contractual requirement (see below);*
   - *Business associates remain contractually liable for other requirements of the business associate agreement.*

b. *Security Official will use the BUSINESS ASSOCIATE DECISION CHART to determine vendor's business associate status Many of the verification steps can/should be used for any contractor.*

c. *Covered Entity shall verify prospective contractor or business associate status by requesting Certificate of Good Standing issued by the Ohio Secretary of State or similar document issued by State Official in your State, certifying good standing of the prospective partner.*

d. Covered Entity shall request a proof of professional liability insurance (not just general slip and fall insurance) and proof of workers compensation coverage for its employees (when applicable).

e. Covered Entity shall request clear statement from vendor describing PHI access needs and how the PHI will be handled.

f. Covered Entity shall request written Statement of Compliance with HIPAA Privacy and Security regulations from business associate, signed by organization CEO/President. Asking that the Business Associate CEO/President personally signs the business associate agreements helps assure that the safeguards are in place.

g. In some instances (e.g. high value/impact agreements, resources available) Covered Entity may want to review the potential business associate Risk Analysis summary report before signing contract and make sure that the PHI is adequately protected. When reviewing the vendor Risk Analysis report special attention shall be placed on:

- *How current the Risk Analysis is (no more than 12 months old), and if it was performed by credentialed vendor (3rd party versus internal self-assessment);*
- *How current is the vendor's associates HIPAA awareness training, is it documented;*
- *Does the vendor have a Risk Management Plan in place, does it address the risks identified in the Risk Analysis;*
- *How high vulnerability risks are being addressed before Business Associate agreement is signed.*
- *Consider incorporating the BA monitoring process (if needed) by requesting monthly BA_DEVICE_REPORT updates identifying ePHI in BA possession, where they reside and how are they protected.*

h. The business associate written agreements shall incorporate the HHS guidance, yet should be customized to reflect particular Covered Entity and vendor specific relationship. The obligations and activities of the business associate, and the use of PHI by business associate, shall reflect the specific vendor need as it relates to service to be provided. Incorporating the "right to audit" the business associate is strongly recommended.

i. Covered Entity shall use the BA_AGREEMENT_TEMPLATE to draft respective agreements with business associates, incorporate "chain of command" for breach notification by business associates and their subcontractors, and specify expense responsibilities.

j. When vendor drafted business associate agreement is used, the Covered Entity will thoroughly review the agreement and will follow recommendations from item (g) of this procedure to limit and/or avoid "boiler plate" language related to use of PHI not applicable to particular business relationship.

k. See additional guidance for:

- *Verifying business status under Workforce Security.*
- *Subpoena triggered Records Release request and BA relationship and consult with legal counsel as needed.*

VII. FACILITY ACCESS CONTROLS

The purpose of these policies and procedures is to limit physical access to Covered Entity or business associate electronic information systems and the facility or facilities in which they are housed, while ensuring that properly authorized access is allowed. All physical safeguards requirements apply to business associates in the same way they apply to covered entities.

A. **Contingency Operations (A)** In case of emergency or incident/disaster access to organization facility may be necessary outside of regular business hours to e.g. restore lost data under the disaster recovery plan and emergency mode operations plan.

Procedure:
Security Official shall be notified about such events and the Security Official shall be contacted to authorize and implement access (e.g. give keys, access code) to the Covered Entity facility. The Security Official has the authority to grant and revoke emergency access to selected individuals, and shall record their names, privileges, who requested access authority and access timeframes as soon as possible.

B. **Facility Security Plan (A)** The policy purpose is to protect and safeguard the Covered Entity facility and the equipment from unauthorized physical access, tampering, and theft. All Covered Entity Workforce shall protect and safeguard the Covered Entity assets. Security Official will be responsible monitoring of the policy implementation.

Procedure:

a. Everyone shall pay attention to locking cabinets with ePHI or Confidential Information, locking doors and windows after hours;

b. Workforce shall exercise vigilance about Covered Entity property and shall report to Security Official immediately any incidents, theft, unauthorized access or tampering with Covered Entity property and especially with information systems components;

c. Doors to the waiting room shall be locked at the end of each business day, [PERSON TITLA/NAME] is responsible for facility lockdown;

d. *Doors between the waiting and service areas shall be locked so they could only be opened from the service area, and access to the service area shall be monitored from the front desk;*
e. *Any additional entrance doors (non-monitored) to the facility shall always be locked so they only are opened form inside by authorized workforce or in emergency situation;*
f. *Any suspicious individuals wondering around the facility shall be confronted and asked about the purpose of being within the facility;*
g. *All non-patients and non-workforce individuals shall sign-in at the front desk (sign-in sheet shall document entry). Visitor's name, company and access time will be recorded in the sign-in sheet at the front desk. When sign-in sheet not used all visitors have to be accompanied by staff when entering practice beyond waiting area.*
h. *All workforce staff shall sign in their respective timesheets when coming in or leaving the facility.*
i. *Facility repairs and modifications shall be documented (scope, date and by whom).*
j. *When security monitoring systems are used (e.g. CCTV), Security Official will determine who has access to these systems and recording media, and frequency of media retention and reuse.*

C. **Access Control and Validation Procedures (A)** Access to Covered Entity facilities and systems will be controlled so only authorized individuals will be granted access. Workforce members will have access to facility based on their roles and functions.

D. ***Procedures:***

a. *Scheduled patients will have access to facility when accompanied by workforce members, their access will be recorded in Practice Management (scheduling) application.*
b. *All other visitors will be granted access to Covered Entity facility by front desk staff upon Security Official permission, and when accompanied by workforce. Staff needs to authenticate visitors identity e.g. delivery or pickup personnel (if allowed on premises where access to IT equipment or PHI is possible) by requesting government issued photo ID, asking for purpose of the visit and accompany the visitor.*
c. *Only Security Official can grant access to Covered Entity information systems or to software programs for testing and revision. Workforce needs to check with Security*

Official for explicit permission before allowing individual's access to their PCs or software.

d. *Workforce access to facility areas containing protected or confidential information or sensitive/critical equipment (e.g. server room, media storage room, executive, HR manager, security official offices) is restricted to respective staff members. Access restriction shall be enforced with locking doors.*

E. **Maintenance records (A)** All repairs and modifications to the physical components of a facility which are related to security (for example, hardware, walls, doors, and locks) will be documented through contracts with vendors.

Procedure:

a. *Repairs and modifications documentation related to information systems will be reviewed and retained by Security Official.*

b. *Contractor's access will be documented through sign-in sheet when individuals enter Covered Entity facility.*

VIII. WORKSTATION SECURITY

A. **Workstation Use (R)** The purpose of this policy is to safeguard protected information and information infrastructure through safe use of the Covered Entity information systems and devices. All workforce members are responsible for implementation of this policy.

Procedure:

a. *The Covered Entity may employ systems and tools to monitor the devices use. End users shall understand that their use of organization devices and systems may be recorded to assure proper functioning of safeguards.*

b. *The Covered Entity information systems and equipment (e.g. computers, storage devices, printers, software and applications) are to be used for business purposes in serving the interests of the Covered Entity, and of its clients and customers in the course of normal operations.*

c. *Users shall be aware that the data they create on the Covered Entity systems remains the property of the Covered Entity. The management must monitor use of Covered Entity resources and cannot guarantee users privacy or the confidentiality of information stored on any device belonging to Covered Entity.*

d. *Workforces is responsible for exercising good judgment regarding the reasonableness of personal use and limit the use of internet, email, blog or social media during work hours using Covered Entity resources. User shall exercise sound judgment in using email, social networking or subscribing to newsgroups and shall not disclose PHI and/or Confidential information about patients or Covered Entity. Business credential/email shall only be used for business related subscriptions.*

e. *Workforce must use extreme caution when opening e-mail attachments received from unknown senders, or downloading files from the internet which may contain malicious software. Users must pay close attention to antivirus/antispyware software warnings.*
f. *Workforce shall maintain clean desk policy and do not store sensitive files in the open; shall tidy up their desks at the end of the working day; shall consider scanning paper documents and filing them on their computers, and following data retention/destruction policies.*
g. *Workstation access will be granted following the Workforce Security and Information Access Management.*
h. *Mobile computing or storage devices not belonging to Covered Entity shall not be connected to Covered Entity network without explicit permission. Storage devices e.g. portable hard drives or USB drives from unknown sources shall not be connected to Covered Entity equipment. Security Official may permit exceptions from this policy.*
i. *External media (e.g. DVD, CD, non-encrypted flash drives) shall not be used for storing PHI. When external media is used for storing Confidential Information, media shall be clearly labeled and protected.*
j. *Users must never install, uninstall or disable software on Covered Entity equipment without explicit permission from Security Official.*

B. **Workstation Security (R)** The purpose of this policy is to safeguard protected information and information infrastructure through secure configuration of the Covered Entity information systems and devices. All workforce members are responsible for implementation of this policy.

Procedure:

a. *Security Official in collaboration with IT and business stakeholders shall establish devices' secure configuration standard(s) by following Center for Internet Security (CIS) standards.*
b. *Minimum security standards shall be enforced by OS and shall include:*
   - *Authorized users are responsible for the security of their passwords and accounts. Passwords shall be changed at least every 90 -120 days, shall be kept secure and not shared. Strong password requirements are enforced.*
   - *Screen savers with passwords to protect unattended machines must be enabled on all Covered Entity computer*

equipment. The screen savers shall turn on after no more than 5 minutes of inactivity. Users shall follow password guidance for implementing passwords described in Section V paragraph A.

- *Automatic log off shall be enabled on all information systems containing ePHI. The automatic logoff shall be activated after 5 minutes of application inactivity.*
- *Installation of unauthorized/unapproved software or applications is prohibited. Users will be held accountable for all actions performed on the system with their User ID. Log on and system events audit logs shall be enabled.*
- *User Access Controls (UAC) shall be enabled, Auto Run for all devices shall be disabled, secure web browser configuration shall be enabled.*
- *Host based firewall and OS auto updates shall be enabled, anti-virus and anti-malware protection shall always be enabled.*

c. *Workstations (PCs) must be secured against use by unauthorized individuals e.g. password protected, cable locks on laptops, PCs positioned to minimize unauthorized viewing of PHI.*

d. *The user must log off or lock/secure the information system when leaving it.*

e. *Server(s) containing PHI or Confidential Information must be installed in a secure area to prevent theft, destruction, or access by unauthorized individuals.*

f. *Portable devices e.g. laptop, smartphones, hard or flash drives (removable media) containing PHI shall always be encrypted and password protected. Portable devices shall never be left unattended in unsecure areas e.g. inside the car in a parking lot/garage. See additional guidance about use of removable media. The loss or theft of portable devices shall be immediately reported to Security Official.*

g. *When portable devices are used offsite users shall exercise additional precautions when accessing PHI.*

- *Do not use public wireless networks for accessing PHI;*
- *Never lose sight of your portable device;*
- *Always log off or lock your device after use;*

IX. DEVICE AND MEDIA CONTROLS

These policies and procedures govern the receipt and removal of hardware and electronic media that contain electronic protected health information into and out of a facility, and the movement of these items within the facility. All hardware and media moves, as well as use of removable media (e.g. USB flash drives) must be coordinated with Security Official to ensure adequate data safeguards

A. **Use of removable media** Inventory controls and best practices will be used to protect organization information systems and data.

Procedure:

a. *Only approved devices and media e.g.* ***USB/flash drives, SD/CF memory cards or external hard drives*** *will be used within the organization. Security Official shall coordinate device/media approval.*
b. *All media and equipment acquisitions and disposal have to be recorded in inventory management e.g. RM-7 HARDWARE form.*
c. *Employees shall never use personal removable media to store and/or transport documents containing ePHI without Security Official permission. Only practice issued, encrypted removable devices shall be used.*
d. *Security Official will determine whether only self-encrypting flash drives will be permissible or whether other storage devices can be used. In such case Security Official will determine which data will be encrypted.*
e. *Employees shall never connect third party removable media to organization computers without Security Official permission.*
f. *Security Official will approve the appropriateness of sharing/accessing practice data on third party systems.*

B. **Disposal (R)** All Protected Health Information (PHI) in non-electronic (e.g. paper) or electronic format, and/or the hardware or electronic media on which it is stored, shall be disposed of and/or erased in such a way which makes the PHI unreadable and unusable.

Procedure:

a. *When workforce determines that work documents e.g. PHI printouts, photo negatives or other paper and microforms documents containing PHI or confidential information, are not required to be retained, these documents need to be destroyed immediately after use. These documents must be shredded. CD/DVD media containing PHI or Confidential information, but no longer needed must be shredded as well.*
b. *Outsourcing device or document destruction services may be an economical approach. Look for a certified vendor with e.g. National Association for Information Destruction (NAID) certification who can provide adequate chain of custody and destruction/sanitization documentation e.g. a certificate of destruction.*
c. *For PHI stored on internal/external storage devices (e.g. computer or printer hard drives, USB/flash drives, memory cards) the Security Official will determine, implement and document proper disposal or sanitization*

method using SANITIZATION FORM. Following alternatives will be considered:

- *Removal (as needed) of the electronic media and its physical destruction by breaking, cutting or pulverizing.*
- *Clearing media by using software to overwrite media with non-sensitive data or executing Secure Erase (ATA drives only). Keep in mind that deleting or re-formatting drives is not a sufficient method to erase/clear electronic media.*
- *Purging media by degaussing/demagnetizing media or using other industry best practices to erase data. Degaussing will make the drive permanently unusable.*

C. **Media re-use (R)** PHI shall be securely removed from electronic media before the media are made available for re-use.

Procedure:

Before reusing electronic media containing PHI e.g. reusing backup drive containing unencrypted PHI, selling PC used to store or access PHI to an employee after PC reached its useful life, the Security Official shall erase/overwrite the PHI data on these devices. This step must be documented using SANITIZATION_FORM.

a. *File deletion or disk formatting is not sufficient for of erasing PHI. Drives containing PHI shall be completely overwritten with non-sensitive data.*
b. *When using USB drives, after inserting them into your computer USB port, Scan it with your Anti-Virus/Anti-Malware software before use. USB virus and malware infestation is quite common.*
c. *Use separate USB for use on public computers at Kinkos, Staples etc.*

D. **Accountability (A)** Information systems inventory records of hardware and electronic media and any person responsible for them will be maintained to enforce accountability. All acquisitions and disposal of equipment will be recorded.

Procedure:

a. *Upon acquisition of information system equipment, the Security Official will notify individual responsible for keeping track of inventory, to update the hardware inventory document (e.g. RM-7_HARDWARE) with appropriate entries/data, to identify whether device contains PHI and who is assigned the device (e.g. individual, department).*
b. *When devices are designated for disposal, the Security Official will complete sanitization/disposal documentation and notify individual responsible for keeping track of inventory to complete the disposal and to update the hardware inventory document.*

E. **Data backup and storage (A)** A retrievable, exact copy of ePHI will be created, as needed, before movement or disposal of equipment.

Procedure:
Security Official will create a retrievable, exact copy of ePHI, as needed, before movement or disposal of equipment or media. Completion of this step and the location of the backup will be recorded in the SANITIZATION_FORM.

X. ACCESS AND AUDIT CONTROLS

The access control policies and procedures for electronic information systems maintain electronic protected health information to allow access only to those persons or software programs that have been granted access rights as specified in Section IV Workforce Security and Information Access Management Policy. All technical safeguards requirements apply to business associates in the same way they apply to covered entities.

A. **Unique User Identification (R) 164.312(a)(2)(i)** Every workforce member accessing ePHI will be assigned a unique User ID allowing the information system to log and track users' activity.

Procedure:
Security Official or designated IT administrator will create unique user accounts for all staff members to access Covered Entity systems or devices. Use of shared accounts shall be strongly discouraged. However, in situations when use of shared account is inevitable (e.g. legacy systems) following shall be implemented:

a. *Security Official justifies why shared account is used;*
b. *Only Security Official can expand shared account usage to new users;*
c. *All shared account users are listed/documented;*
d. *Shared account password is changed more frequently e.g. every 60 days. Password is always changed when user sharing account is removed (e.g. employee termination).*

B. **Emergency Access Procedure (R) 164.312(a)(2)(ii)** Security Official can grant access to ePHI in emergency situation.

Procedure:
Requests for emergency access shall be directed to Security Official who can assign a unique User ID allowing the information system to log and track users' activity Security Official shall record users' names, privileges, who requested access authority and access timeframes as soon as possible. Access granted in emergency situations shall be removed/deleted as soon as

possible after the need for access no longer exists. Access removal shall be recorded (when, and who removed access).

C. **Automatic Logoff (A) 164.312(a)(2)(iii)** Automatic logoff feature (when available) shall be enabled on all systems providing access to or containing ePHI.

Procedure:
Automatic log off shall be enabled on all information systems containing ePHI. The automatic logoff shall be activated after 5 minutes of application inactivity. Automatic logoff for smartphones shall be no longer than 1 minute.

D. **Encryption and Decryption (A) 164.312(a)(2)(iv)** Device and/or data encryption shall be incorporated to protect ePHI and sensitive data. Security Official shall identify all devices/data to be encrypted and backup location of encryption keys. Data transmission, disk or file encryption methodologies need to be Federal Information Processing Standards FIPS 140-2 validated.

Procedure:
Security Official will develop data/information classification matrix to classify sensitivity and protection levels for different types of data. The matrix should also include directions for storing or encrypting the data e.g.

	Secret	***Confidential***	***Public***
Data examples	*passwords, credit card numbers, SSN, merger and acquisition plans*	*ePHI, master patient index numbers, insurance and bank account numbers, system configuration information, detail financial records, vulnerability scan reports, internal memos, user directories, system or end-user documentation, inventories*	*press releases, brochures, annual reports*
Electronic Storage	*Must be always encrypted*	*ePHI- must be encrypted; Access controls required*	*No restrictions*
Mobile devices and email	*Must never be stored on mobile devices, never emailed*	*Access controls required, emailed only to authorized recipients with secure email*	*No restrictions*
Hard copy storage	*Double locked in authorized locations only*	*Locked*	*No restrictions*

Destruction	*Physical drive destruction, degaussing or overwriting drives with random data, cross cut shred, destruction documented with e.g. sanitization form.*	*Physical drive destruction, degaussing or overwriting drives with random data, cross cut shred,*	*No restrictions*

All mobile devices accessing, storing or processing Secret or Confidential data have to be encrypted with whole disk encryption.

a. *The Security Official will identify FIPS compliant (e.g. AES) encryption methodology, and devices and files/folders which will be encrypted. In general, entire devices containing ePHI and Confidential Information (including mobile and removable media) shall be encrypted. Security Official will follow specific device or software manufacturer (e.g. Microsoft BitLocker solution), or IT professional guidance/help in encrypting devices.*
b. *When encryption of the entire device is not possible, files and folders containing ePHI or confidential data shall be encrypted. Certain Operating Systems like Windows 7 or software packages allow for file encryption. Keep in mind that file-level encryption does NOT give you the "safe harbor" protection in case of security incident involving loss of device/data. The whole disk/device encryption shall be used for safe transport of the data.*
c. *Security Official will determine files and folders to be encrypted, will instruct users how to encrypt files (see # 4 below) and will back up user encryption keys for data decryption in case of equipment or media failure. Users shall exercise good judgment and encrypt files containing ePHI or Confidential Information identified for encryption.*
d. *Encryption and decryption procedures and key management (backup) will be defined for specific technologies used by Security Official.*
e. *Data transmission encryption procedures (server, email) will be defined per specific technologies used by Security Official.*

E. **Audit Controls (A) 164.312(b)** Systems containing ePHI will have the system activity logging/tracking features enabled, when these features are available. The audit logs will be reviewed by Security Official as identified and scheduled in the Risk Management Plan, Section III (C) and Information System Activity Review.

Procedure:
Security Official will review and enable system's auditing capabilities.

a. *Data should be logged when possible based on assigned access roles and shall include: Unique user ID, log in date/time, activities performed within the system e.g. viewing, data entry or modification, report creation, policy changes, account creation/ deletion, transaction processing and approval.*
b. *At minimum system (and or desktop) audit logs shall be enabled to audit logon events, account logon events and system logon events. The log file size shall be sufficient to retain audit data for at least 3 months. Security official will determine frequency of logs review.*

F. **Integrity - Mechanism to Authenticate Electronic Protected Health Information (A) 164.312(c)(1), 164.312(c)(2)**

Data integrity (error free data) needs to be maintained by the organization in all systems, databases and documentation.

Procedure:
Following approaches will be used to assure data integrity and to authenticate ePHI:

a. *Security Official will verify that access controls to systems are enforced throughout the organization (unique user IDs, passwords). Security Official will verify per system activity review schedule;*
b. *Electronic data is signed before sending, emails use digital signatures; Office 365 Information Rights Management is used;*
c. *Encrypted and redundant data (database) backup will be maintained following data backup procedures and schedules;*
d. *Billing transactions will be reconciled on a monthly basis.*

G. **Person or Entity Authentication (R) 164.312(d)**

Strictly controlled passwords will be used as described in Section V (A) Security Awareness and Training Log-in and Password management. Users will be held accountable for all actions performed on the system with their User ID. Biometric readers will be phased in when feasible. Two-factor authentication will be used to access data or systems containing data classified as Secret. Multifactor authentication will be used for remote system access, for Cloud systems administration etc.

Procedure:
Security Official will assure implementation of secure configuration for computing devices by following review schedule e.g. policy compliance scans, review of password policies for network devices, review of system(s) and devices user lists, account creation and access granting policies and assignments.

H. **Transmission Security - Integrity Controls (A) 164.312(e)(1), 164.312(e)(2)(i)**

Confidentiality and integrity of ePHI and confidential data will be protected during transmission.

Procedure:

Security Official will assure proper network configuration and system connections for data transmission, so the ePHI and confidential data is only transmitted through secure, encrypted connections using e.g. TLS protocols.

a. *EHR/PM systems' capabilities to transmit data between systems in encrypted format will be utilized. Authorized staff will follow system vendor's procedures to assure secure configuration of transmission protocols;*
b. *ePHI data files can only be transported when they are encrypted. Keep in mind that file-level encryption does NOT give you the "safe harbor" protection in case of security incident involving loss of data (devices). The whole disk/device encryption shall be used for safe transport of the data. Transmission of documents containing PHI (mailing to patients) has to be reviewed and approved by authorized staff.*
c. *Encrypted and redundant data backup will be maintained.*
d. *Billing transactions will be reconciled on a monthly basis;*
e. *Email encryption will be used for sending PHI or confidential information. Digital Certificate based signatures will be used for electronic communications and document protection. Office 365 encryption or Information Rights Management will be used to protect sensitive documents. Password protection and encryption will be used for documents containing PHI or confidential information.*

I. **Transmission Security - Encryption (A) 164.312(e)(2)(ii)**

Confidentiality and integrity of ePHI and confidential data will be protected during transmission.

Procedure:

a. *On line data backup, data transmission between systems, transaction processing and data transmission between servers and web based clients will use secure, encrypted network connections employing VPN or TLS protocols.*

b. *Data stored on devices or transported on devices will be encrypted. Disk level encryption and file level encryption shall be used as appropriate and as determined by Security Official.*

XI. SECURITY POLICIES AND PROCEDURES

Security policies and procedures describe standards and provide necessary rule sets and governance structure to the organization.

A. Business Associate Contracts or Other Arrangements – Implementation specifications (R) (164.314(a)(1))

The Covered Entity will determine their contractor's/partner's business associate status and implement Business Associate Agreements for entities categorized as Business Associates

Procedure:

Security Official will use Business Associate procedures from Section VI (H) procedures will be used to assure proper implementation of this policy, and must assure specific contract language addressing data safeguards, contract termination, data breach notifications and subcontractors' requirements. Requirements of this section §164.314 apply to business associates' subcontractors, as subcontractors are directly responsible for safeguarding ePHI.

Business associates are responsible for assuring HIPAA safeguards implementation at subcontractor level through business associate agreements.

B. Policies and Procedures and Documentation Requirements

Policies and Procedures (R)

The Covered Entity or business associate will create, maintain and implement appropriate Policies and Procedures to comply with HIPAA Privacy and Security standards. The Covered Entity or business associate will document any changes to their Policy and Procedures.

Procedure:

a. *Security Official will periodically initiate policies and procedures review and updates, to verify that actual activities are accurately reflected in policies and procedures. Policy and procedures changes will be documented by providing last revision date and name of the individual making revisions. Documentation review shall be initiated at least:*

- *During the risk assessment process;*
- *During system or business process redesign or new technologies implementation;*
- *When regulatory changes occur;*

b. *Changes can be implemented when it is reasonable and appropriate at any time.*

C. **Policies and Procedures and Documentation Requirements**

Documentation (R)

The Covered Entity or business associate will maintain Policies and Procedures in written format (may be electronic). Covered Entity or business associate will maintain written documentation for actions, assessments and activities described in the Policies and Procedures, which need to be documented.

Procedure:
Security Official will assure following:

Time limit (R) - Covered Entity or business associate will retain the documentation required in this section for 6 years from the date of its creation or the date when it last was in effect, whichever is later.
Availability (R) - Covered Entity or business associate will make documentation available to those persons responsible for implementing the procedures to which the documentation pertains.
Updates (R) - Covered Entity or business associate will review documentation periodically (at least annually), and update as needed, in response to environmental or operational changes affecting the security of the electronic protected health information.

D. **Electronic signatures**

Electronic signatures will be utilized for any and all records in the organization when applicable to automate the document processing (signing) and strengthen the authentication of the signor. Computer generated, transcribed documents and electronic entries can be authenticated with electronic/digital signatures. System generated signatures will be considered legally binding when time can be verified and signor/author of the electronic entry can be authenticated.

Procedure:

a. *Electronic signatures can be used wherever handwritten signatures are used unless prohibited by law.*
b. *All using electronic signatures are to review documents and all entries before applying electronic signature. Document/ record changes after electronic signature has been applied will*

be prevented by the computer system. Any changes or addendums to the original document must also be signed electronically and time stamped.

c. *Application and system specific standards may vary by system/application. The security officer will select and formally approve use of specific tools/applications for electronic signatures. Following document signing applications/tools are often used: DocuSign, Adobe Echosign, Signix, digital certificates issued by Certification Authority.*
d. *When digital certificates are used for electronic signatures, these digital certificates shall be issued by independent Certification Authority. Use of self-signed digital certificates shall be avoided.*
e. *Auditing electronic signatures/record entries must incorporate secure, computer-generated, time-stamped audit trail preventing modification of the original record entries or signatures. Record changes shall not obscure previously recorded information. Audit information shall be retained for at least the same period the original record needs to be retained.*

XII. PRIVACY POLICIES AND PROCEDURES

Sections 164.500 - 164.532 address privacy rules, patient's rights, and disclosure's limitations, the most important privacy provisions are explained below and in privacy forms/templates. Please note that Business Associates (BA) are directly liable under the HIPAA Privacy Rules:

- For impermissible uses and disclosures
- For a failure to provide access to a copy of electronic protected health information to either the covered entity, the individual, or the individual's designee (whichever is specified in the business associate agreement),
- For a failure to disclose protected health information where required by the Secretary,
- For a failure to provide an accounting of disclosures,
- For applying minimum necessary standard when disclosing PHI.

In general business associates are not required to designate privacy official or provide notice of privacy practices unless such responsibility is delegated to business associate as a contractual requirement, please see Business Associate procedure for additional details.

Procedure:

Security Official will assure the following policy elements and procedures are implemented:

A. ***Notice of Privacy Practices*** *(NPP) should be available for patients at all times. NPP should be posted in service location and printed copies shall be available for immediate pickup. Front desk staff shall provide all patients with the Notice of Privacy Practices (NPP) and all forms supporting patients' rights upon patients' request. Please see the Notice of Privacy Practices template for summary of patient's rights and examples of disclosures permitted by law. The NPP should help you answer most of the patient's questions.*

B. *Front desk staff shall ask each patient if she/he was offered the Notice of Privacy Practices. Staff shall collect the NPP_ACKNOWLEDGEMENT_RECEIPT and retain it with patient record e.g. scan it and attach it to electronic record. Alternative solution is to maintain a log (could be electronic) where patient acknowledges with signature that she/he was offered the NPP.*

C. *All patients' forms listed in this section, and other used/submitted by patients need to be filled with patients' record (could be scanned and attached in electronic format).*

D. *Request for access to health information, request for accounting of PHI disclosure, personal representative designations and request to amend health information have to be submitted on practice specific forms, have to be signed by requesting individual and approved by Security Official. Each of these forms provides brief policy overview for you and for the patient. Please read it and follow it.*

E. *Deceased patient information is protected for 50 years following the death of individual and proper authorization is provided when record is requested.*

F. ***Email communication.*** *Patient Consent for Electronic Communication needs to be obtained before we can communicate with patient via email.*

   a. *Security Official will determine the scope and purpose of email communications with patients: limited scope may only include appointment reminders (non-encrypted communications), full scope may include all ePHI (encrypted communications).*

   b. *All outgoing email shall include following email privacy notice at the end: "This message contains information that may be confidential or privileged. The information is intended solely for the recipient and its use by any other party is not authorized. If you are not the intended recipient, be aware that any disclosure, copying, distribution or use of the contents of this information is prohibited. Please notify the sender if you received this email in error and delete the original."*

   c. *Ask patient if they feel comfortable with email communications, emphasize the limited purpose of these communications just to inform them about meeting schedules or the convenience and security of these communications when encrypted email or Secure Email Account is used. Use CONSENT FOR ELECTRONIC COMMUNICATION FORM to document patients' agreement to use email communications and to document their acknowledgement of associated risks. Demonstrate the use of secure email if possible.*

d. *Patients may choose to receive ePHI in non-encrypted emails. This patient choice shall be documented in CONSENT_FOR_ELECTRONIC_COMMUNICATION_FORM.*

It is NOT recommended to use this option because:

- *Sending ePHI in open email may be perceived that the provider does not care about securing patients information.*
- *Exceptions from sending ePHI only in encrypted format may create confusion and inconsistencies in employee behaviors potentially leading to data breaches.*
- *It may still be costly to investigate and prove whose fault lead to data breach.*

G. ***Patient Access to the Medical Record****. Patients have the right to access their personal health information including its electronic format. We may deny (without right to review) patient access to PHI if:*

a. *PHI contains psychotherapy notes;*

b. *PHI is gathered to prepare for and use in a civil, criminal or administrative proceeding, PHI is subject to CLIA 1988;*

c. *PHI is for an inmate at a correctional facility.*

The patient can appeal the denial and ask for review by another licensed health professional designated by the practice if:

- *A licensed health care professional has determined that access to your personal health information is likely to endanger your safety or the safety of another person;*
- *Your personal health information refers to another person.*

Patients may inspect personal health information at our office, or they may have a copy of their personal health information sent to them in hard copy or electronic format. They may be charged a reasonable, cost-based fee for copies of their health records (based on actual cost, average cost or flat rate fee methodology described at http://www.hhs.gov/hipaa/for-professionals/privacy/guidance/access/index.html#maximu mflatfee, or fees based on Medical Records Fees established by provider or in some states regulatory organizations e.g. http://www.nosscr.org/state-medical-records-payment-rates

(use appropriate State schedule when costs are same as those permitted under HIPAA – reasonable/cost based). In general fees can only reflect costs of copying records and/or creating summary/explanation of the information, but not record searching and retrieval cost. Cost of supplies can be added to the fee (paper, postage, CD).

REQUEST_FOR_ACCESS_TO_HEALTH_INFORMATION form shall be used for this request.

Access to patient information has to be provided within 30 days from request date. A one-time, 30 days extension for responding to individual's request can be used. Patient has to be notified about extension in wiring and the reasons for delay and extension has to be explained in writing as well.

H. ***Authorization to disclose health information*** *§164.508-164.510. Protected health information (PHI) will only be released from our practice with a properly executed authorization from the patient or his/her personal representative. Authorizations must be properly executed by the patient or his personal representative. The AUTHORIZATION_TO_DISCLOSE_INFORMATION form has to be used. PHI including psychotherapy notes shall not be disclosed or used for marketing purposes, or disclosures that constitute sale of PHI, without authorization.* ***Authorization is not needed*** *when PHI is shared with another physician/ healthcare professional participating in continuum of patient care. For example, patient's ophthalmologist doesn't need patient authorization to share exam results or treatment suggestions with primary care physician; an oncology practice doesn't need the patient authorization to share information with primary care physician. When other medical professional/ practice calls and asks your practice about patient's PHIs, and this professional is NOT on the record as patient's healthcare provider,* ***validity of the request shall be verified with patient*** *- call the patient and ask. NPP provides additional information about how we use PHI and how we may use or disclose PHI without authorization. Here are few authorization issues worth noting:*

   a. ***Proof of immunization to schools.*** *Covered entity can disclose, with the oral or written agreement of a parent or guardian, a child's proof of immunization to schools in States that have school entry or similar laws. Written request, in form of email or a phone call followed by note in child's school medical record is sufficient. The parent/guardian signature is not required.*

   b. *For certain research studies authorization to use and disclose PHI will be needed. HIPAA Final Rule allows for compound authorization, thus eliminating need for multiple forms and allowing participants to authorize future research uses and disclosures at time of initial authorization.*

c. *Authorization to disclose decedent's PHI is not needed for individuals who have been deceased for more than 50 years. To clarify the PHI protection period is not a record retention requirement.*

d. *Authorization to disclose decedent's PHI to family members or others involved in individual's healthcare or payment for healthcare is not needed. Providers are permitted, but not required to share this information unless doing so would be inconsistent with prior expressed preference of the individual.*

I. ***HIPAA Privacy and Disclosures in Emergency Situations.*** *Patient information can be shared:*

a. *To provide treatment e.g. sharing with other providers, referring for treatment, coordinating care with others (e.g. emergency relief workers);*

b. *To seek payment for services;*

c. *To identify, locate and notify family members, guardians, or anyone else responsible for the individual's care of the individual's location, general condition, or death (hospital can notify police, press etc. to identify or locate family members).*

Disaster relief organizations that are authorized by law or by their charters to assist in disaster relief efforts can share information when responding to emergency;

d. *To prevent or lessen a serious and imminent threat to the health and safety of a person or the public;*

e. *Health care facilities maintaining a directory of patients can tell people who call or ask about individuals whether the individual is at the facility, their location in the facility, and general condition.*

J. ***PHI disclosure to law enforcement****. In all cases, authenticity of the document requesting PHI shall be reviewed and verified (take time to examine the document).*

Identity of the requestor/officer must be verified before release of information as well. Individuals shall ask for identification <u>and examine it</u>, do not allow the ID to be just flashed.

Copies of all related documents must be retained. Except when required by law, the disclosures to law enforcement summarized below are subject to a <u>minimum necessary</u>

<u>disclosure</u> (only disclose minimum information necessary to satisfy requestor objective). In general disclosures for law enforcement purposes are permitted as follows:

a. *To comply with a court order or court-ordered warrant, a subpoena or summons issued by a judicial officer, or a grand jury subpoena;*

b. *To respond to an administrative request without judicial involvement. The administrative request should include a written statement that the information requested is relevant and material, specific and limited in scope, and de-identified information cannot be used. Make sure the request is signed and dated, and you recognize the organization, verify as needed.*

c. *To respond to a request for PHI for purposes of identifying or locating a suspect, fugitive, material witness or missing person. However, the covered entity must limit disclosures of PHI to: name, address, date and place of birth, social security number, ABO blood type and rh factor, type of injury, date and time of treatment, date and time of death, and a description of distinguishing physical characteristics. Other information related to the individual's DNA, dental records, body fluid or tissue typing, samples, or analysis <u>cannot</u> be disclosed under this provision, but may be disclosed in response to a court order, warrant, or written administrative request.*

d. This same limited information (listed above) may be reported to law enforcement:

- *About a suspected perpetrator of a crime when the report is made by the victim who is a member of the covered entity's workforce;*
- *To identify or apprehend an individual who has admitted participation in a violent crime that the covered entity reasonably believes may have caused serious physical harm to a victim, provided that the admission was not made in the course of or based on the individual's request for therapy, counseling, or treatment related to the propensity to commit this type of violent act.*

e. To respond to a request for PHI about a victim of a crime, and when the victim agrees.

- *Child abuse or neglect may be reported to any law enforcement official authorized by law to receive such reports and the agreement of the individual is not required.*
- *Adult abuse, neglect, or domestic violence may be reported to a law enforcement official authorized by law*

to receive such reports if: the individual agrees; report required by law; expressly authorized by law, to prevent harm or in certain emergency situations.

f. *To report PHI to law enforcement when required by law (e.g. gunshots, stab wounds).*

g. *To alert law enforcement to the death of the individual, when there is a suspicion that death resulted from criminal conduct. Information about a decedent may also be shared with medical examiners or coroners.*

h. *To report PHI that the covered entity in good faith believes to be evidence of a crime that occurred on the covered entity's premises.*

i. *When responding to an off-site medical emergency, as necessary to alert law enforcement about criminal activity.*

j. *To a law enforcement official reasonably able to prevent or lessen a serious and imminent threat to the health or safety of an individual or the public.*

k. *To identify or apprehend an individual who appears to have escaped from lawful custody.*

l. *For certain other specialized governmental law enforcement purposes, such as:*

- *To federal officials authorized to conduct intelligence, counter-intelligence, and other national security activities under the National Security Act or to provide protective services to the President and others and conduct related investigations.*
- *To respond to a request for PHI by a correctional institution or a law enforcement official having lawful custody of an inmate or others if they represent such PHI is needed to provide health care to the individual.*

K. ***PHI disclosure for Public Health and research.***

a. *PHI can be disclosed without authorization for public health purposes e.g. to report and prevent spread of diseases, to maintain disease or immunization registries.*

b. *PHI can be disclosed without authorization to support research when privacy and security is assured (limited data sets). See point G for additional information.*

c. *Coroners and medical examiners. A covered entity may disclose protected health information to a coroner or medical examiner for the purpose of identifying a deceased person, determining a cause of death, or other duties as authorized by law. A covered entity that also performs the duties of a coroner or medical examiner may use protected health information for the purposes described above.*

d. *Funeral directors. A covered entity may disclose protected health information to funeral directors, consistent with applicable law, as necessary to carry out their duties with respect to the decedent. If necessary for funeral directors to carry out their duties, the covered entity may disclose the protected health information prior to, and in reasonable anticipation of, the individual's death.*

e. *Uses and disclosures for cadaveric organ, eye or tissue donation purposes. A covered entity may use or disclose protected health information to organ procurement organizations or other entities engaged in the procurement, banking, or transplantation of cadaveric organs, eyes, or tissue for the purpose of facilitating organ, eye or tissue donation and transplantation.*

L. ***Patient Consent to share patient pictures/ photographs****. Patient images, pictures allowing for patient identification cannot be shared without patient's written consent. This policy applies also to sharing patient pictures in social media sites. Please use CONSENT_TO_SHARE_PICTURES form.*

M. ***Medical record amendment****. Any patient may request that his/her medical record be changed, corrected, or amended. The request must be submitted on our REQUEST_TO_AMEND_HEALTH_INFORMATION form.*

We do not have to agree with patient request if the personal health information we have about the patient is accurate and complete, or was not created by us, or is not part of a designated record set, or is not available for patient to see. We are required to respond within 60 days after we receive the request if we will agree to patient request or if we need more time to respond to the request. One 30-day extension is permitted if the patient is notified of the reason for the delay. If the request is denied, the practice must give a reason for denying the request. The patient may file a written rebuttal to the denial which needs to be retained with patient's record. When request is approved the patient needs to complete the PHI Amendment Notification Request section of the REQUEST_TO_AMEND_HEALTH_INFORMATION form. This section is used to notify other healthcare providers about PHI amendment for the patient. Coordinate communications with Privacy/Security Official.

N. ***Patients' requests restricting use of PHI.*** *Patients have the right to ask us to restrict the ways we use and share their PHI for its treatment, payment and health care operations purposes. We are not required to agree with this request for a restriction, but will do our best to accommodate all reasonable requests. The requests will be reviewed and considered by Security Official. REQUEST TO RESTRICT USES AND DISCLOSURES OF HEALTH INFOR-MATION form has to be used.*

O. ***Patient's request restricting disclosure of PHI to a health plan*** *with respect to health care for which patient is paying out of pocket in full. This request has to be made before services are provided. Front desk staff needs to ask patient: "Have you received our Notice of Privacy Practices and ...Will you be using your health plan to pay for services obtained today?"*

   When patient indicates out of pocket payment, and wants to restrict disclosure of care information to health plan:

   - *Full payment for service should be requested/accepted,*
   - *And the EHR/PM system's capabilities need to be used to flag the service/transaction (e.g. use comment field "patient restricts info with health plan"), so services are not billed/send to the health plan.*

   Alternative - could be more efficient, can be used depending on EHR/PM system's functionality and volume of "paid in full at time of service" transactions.

   All transactions involving out of pocket payments in full at time of service should be treated as those restricting disclosure of care information to health plan (should be automatically flagged). Front desk staff after accepting full payment should confirm restriction with patient and "un-flag" the transaction as needed.

   When restrictions are requested the provider cannot disclose the restricted PHI to health plan business associate as well.

P. ***Personal representative designation.*** *Patient can name Personal Representative to receive PHI on behalf of the patient. Personal Representative Designation will last until it is revoked in writing. Any revocation can only apply on and after the date we receive the Revocation. Use PERSONAL REPRESENTATIVE DESIG-NATION form to designate and revoke personal representatives.*

Q. ***Request for an accounting of disclosures of PHI.*** *Patients have the right to ask how we have shared their PHI on and after April 14, 2003. They may request this accounting of all disclosures for a period of time up to six years from the date of the request. You are required to give patient an accounting or the summary of the disclosures, or tell the patient if you* *need more time to respond to the request within 60 days after you receive the request.*

The first accounting or summary in any 12-month period is free. If patient requests more than one accounting or summary in a 12-month period, we can charge a fee for the cost of the copies of the PHI or the cost of preparing the summary.

Disclosures for law enforcement or public health, including student immunization disclosures are subject to accounting. Authorized (authorization form on file), and TPO related disclosures are exempt from accounting for disclosures. Healthcare operations related disclosures when payment is received for disclosed PHI have to be accounted for. Use REQUEST FOR ACCOUNTING OF PHI DISCLOSURE form to accommodate this request.

R. ***Request for alternative communication, to contact client at different address.*** *Patients have the right to ask us to contact them about PHI at a different address or in a different way than we contact them now. These requests are often made when a person feels their health or safety is in danger if PHI is sent to his or her home address. We will do our best to accommodate all reasonable requests. These requests can be approved and completed by front desk staff checking the patient in. Please make sure contact information changes are communicated to staff completing billing etc. REQUEST FOR ALTERNATIVE MEANS OF COMMUNICATION form has to be used.*

S. ***Complaints.***

a. ***Complaint about use of PHI*** *(NPP). Patients have the right to complain in writing about how we, or other people or organizations that work for us, used or shared their personal health information. This complaint must be submitted on our COMPLAINT_EPHI_USE form. The complaint can also be submitted to the U.S. Department of Health and Human Services Secretary. The complaint must be submitted within 180 days of the event of concern. Privacy and Security Official will review and investigate all complaints.*

b. *Patient* ***concerns about services and appointments*** *need to be documented using PATIENT_CONCERN form and directed to Office Manager.*

c. *Complaints will be reviewed by Privacy/Security Official. The documents need to be attached to patients' file (could be electronic). The Security Official will review, investigate and resolve the complaint in coordination with practice leadership, and respond to the patient within 14 business days. The response (even when verbal) needs to be documented in patients' file along with complaint form.*

The workforce, when facing a complaint in a face to face or over the phone situation shall:

- *exhibit extreme courtesy to the patient, be sympathetic,*
- *acknowledge the issues and be understanding of the customer frustration,*
- *listen to the problem and try to be helpful,*
- *offer the complaint form and provide direct contact information,*
- *identify a response time and respond to patient within that time frame, and*
- *offer elevating the issue to Security Official for resolution.*

T. ***Request to opt out of fundraising communications (NPP***). *When covered entity engages in fundraising communications, it can use and disclose certain PHI without individual's authorization. Following PHI elements can be used: demographic information (names, addresses, other contact information, age, gender, and dates of birth), health insurance status, dates of healthcare provided, department of service information (cardiology), treating physician and outcome information. The fundraising communications have to <u>include an opt out option so patients can easily unsubscribe</u> from those communications e.g. toll-free number and/or email.*

U. ***Use of ePHI for marketing or sale of ePHI*** *without patient authorization is strictly prohibited. Marketing is defined as making communications about product or service that encourages patients to purchase or use the product or service.*

V. ***In case of a data breach*** *of unsecure protected health information, a data breach notification has to be provided to affected individuals. When breach is born by business associate or its subcontractor, the breach should be reported to covered entity, who should notify patients - see Business Associates procedure for details.*

W. ***[Health Plans only]*** *All health plans are prohibited from using or disclosing* ***genetic information for underwriting purposes.***

X. *All confidentiality agreements for volunteers have to be attached to volunteers' personnel records.*

Y. ***Records release in response to subpoena*** *- suggested steps.*

This procedure identifies suggested actions/steps when responding to subpoenas for medical records. Please consult your legal counsel in all legal matters.

a. *The Security Official will be responsible for handling and managing all subpoenas for PHI. Security Official will communicate the subpoena request to leadership and will coordinate the response with Covered Entity leadership and legal counsel.*

b. *Security Official will take following steps when managing subpoenas for PHI:*

- *Security Official will determine validity of the request;*
- *Determine the specific PHI elements that need to be released (necessary minimum);*
- *Request that the party issuing the subpoena provide evidence of authorization from the individual whose records are requested (when appropriate);*
- *If authorization not available, determine if Covered Entity should disclose PHI based upon the situation (discovery request or other lawful process).*
- *Ensure the following: there is satisfactory assurance from the party seeking the PHI, that reasonable efforts have been made to ensure that the individual who is the subject of the requested PHI has been given notice of the request. If they cannot provide such assurance, Security Official shall make reasonable efforts to provide notice to the individual, or can object to PHI disclosure.*
- *Ensure there is satisfactory assurance from the party seeking the PHI that reasonable efforts have been made by the party to secure a qualified protective order, as appropriate.*

c. *If Security Official decides that PHI should be disclosed, the best way to provide those items, and no PHI beyond those items, to the requestor shall be determined. Security Official must make reasonable efforts not to disclose more information than is requested.*

d. *Security Official shall ask for assurance that the party requesting the PHI has appropriate safeguards in place for the PHI. This can be accomplished by:*

- *Asking the CEO, legal counsel, or other executive within the requesting organization to sign an attestation indicating safeguards meeting the requirements of the HIPAA Privacy and Security Rule are in place, or by;*
- *Asking to see recent attestation of completion of the information security audit and/or risk assessment that finds privacy and security safeguards are satisfactory.*

These Policies and Procedures apply to all users of Covered Entity systems and data. If not otherwise specified, all workforce members are responsible for adherence to and implementation of the policies listed in this document. The Security Official is responsible for implementation of specific policies, and is responsible for guidance interpretation and/or implementation for all policies.

Any employee found to have violated this policy will be subject to disciplinary actions described in Sanctions Policy, Section III (D), up to and including termination of employment or business relationship. Additional penalties associated with state and federal laws may apply.

Some organizations include EMPLOYEE STANDARDS OF CONDUCT and ETHICS in their policies and procedures, and/or in employee handbook.

ATTACHMENT A
SECURITY OFFICIAL

_______________________________ has been designated the Privacy and Security Official for Covered Entity Name. The Security Official is responsible for assuring appropriate and reasonable implementation of security management practices within the practice to meet HIPAA Privacy and Security Rule Standards.

This designation shall be effective on ____________ until amended or revoked.

The Security Official will be responsible for development, implementation, documentation and monitoring of Risk Management Plan, and policies and procedures implementation, review and updates as needed.

_______________________________ has been designated as a backup/ alternative Security Official for Covered Entity to address Policies and Procedures in absence of primary Security Official.

Specific responsibilities of the Security Official include:

a. Ensuring privacy and security policies, procedures, and standards are in place and adhered to by entity.
b. Providing basic privacy and security support for all systems and users.
c. Providing on-going employee privacy and security education.
d. Performing periodic audits/log review.
e. Managing system(s) users and overseeing information use.
f. Reporting regularly to the Covered Entity Owner on entity's status with regard to HIPAA Privacy and Security compliance.

PRIMARY SECURITY OFFICIAL:

/Printed or Typed Name/	/Signature/	/Date/

COVERED ENTITY:

/Printed or Typed Name/	/Signature/	/Date/

SECONDARY/BACKUP SECURITY OFFICIAL:

/Printed or Typed Name/	/Signature/	/Date/

ATTACHMENT B
Confidentiality Statement and Policy Acknowledgement

I acknowledge that I have been provided the [PRACTICE NAME] General Operations and Information Security Policy and Procedures.

- I have read and understand these policies and procedures, and I understand my responsibility for their implementation.
- I specifically understand my responsibility to maintain privacy, security and confidentiality of Protected Health Information and Confidential Information created, used or transmitted within the [PRACTICE NAME].
- I understand that in case I am found to have violated this policy, I will be subject to disciplinary actions described in Sanctions Policy, Section III, which may result in termination of my employment.
- I understand that additional civil and/or criminal penalties associated with state and federal laws related to privacy and security may apply.

Employee name:	
Employee signature:	
Date:	

Access granted to following systems containing PHI:	
Granted by (name/signature):	
Date:	

This document shall be signed by <u>all Covered Entity Workforce</u> on the first day of workforce employment or engagement, and shall be retained according to HIPAA standard. Accordingly, the appropriate note shall be made in RM-2_WORKFORCE file.

ATTACHMENT C - Personal Mobile Devices Use Agreement

I request permission to use my Personal Mobile Device (PMD) to access PRACTICE NAME systems and data for work-related purposes.

I agree to use my PMD described below in accordance with the PRACTICE NAME General Operations and Information Security Policy and Procedures, and I understand that all Policies and Procedures will apply to this device just like they apply to equipment owned by the PRACTICE NAME. I understand that permission to use my PMD to access PRACTICE NAME systems may be revoked at any time.

I agree to the additional limitations and requirements specific to PMD described below:

1. I will protect the device with strong Password, inactivity time out/log off setting of no more than 5 minutes and best encryption practices possible for my PMD (whole device, application or file encryption). I will use separate Password for application accessing ePHI.
2. I agree to surrender my device immediately to Security Official upon request for review in course of scheduled or unscheduled device monitoring activities, review or investigation.
3. I agree for the PRACTICE NAME to install specific software on my PMD, enabling the PRACTICE NAME:
    a. To manage mobile devices (e.g. track network access, monitor for malicious software or implementation of security policies).
    b. To remotely wipe out the ePHI, Confidential Information or other data belonging to the PRACTICE NAME, in case the device is determined to be compromised (stolen, lost, not with authorized user).
    c. I agree to use only specific applications, selected and approved by Security Official for access to PRACTICE NAME systems or ePHI.
    d. I agree to remove specific applications deemed by Security Official unsecure from my PMD.
4. I agree to hold the PRACTICE NAME harmless from any liability, claims or expenses arising from or in connection with damages to my PMD or loss of personal data stored on my PMD.

Employee name:			
Employee signature:			
Date:			
Device info type/description			
Access granted to following systems containing ePHI:			
Is the device encrypted:	☐ YES		☐ NO
Device access granted to ePHI:	☐ View Only	☐ View & Store	☐ View, Store, Modify
Granted by (name/signature):			
Date:			
Revoked by (name/signature):			
Date:			

This document shall be signed by anyone permitted to use Personal Mobile Device to access Covered Entity systems and data before access is granted and after the ATTACHMENT C – Confidentiality Statement and Policy Acknowledgement is signed. The document shall be retained according to HIPAA standard. Accordingly the appropriate note shall be made in RM-2_WORKFORCE and RM-7_HARDWARE files.

HIPAA SAFEGUARDS Ten Top Things To Remember (revise as needed)

1. Always protect all your devices including mobile devices with Password
2. Never share your Password...
3. Encrypt sensitive data on your devices...Encrypt devices
4. Never leave your mobile devices unattended...Never
5. Never leave sensitive paper data unattended...Never
6. Always log off or lock your device when leaving it unattended or not in use
7. Make sure your device locks or logs off automatically after short period of inactivity.
8. Use built in biometric security features when possible
9. Report incidents immediately
10. When in doubt - do not do it. Check policy, ask Security Official.

Resources

ONC HIT - Comprehensive guide to help professionals and providers understand and incorporate, privacy and security into their practice.
http://www.healthit.gov/providers-professionals/ehr-privacy-security

2013 HIPAA Omnibus Final Rule
http://federalregister.gov/a/2013-01073

Summary of the HIPAA Privacy Rule
http://www.hhs.gov/hipaa/for-professionals/privacy/laws-regulations/index.html

HIPAA Breaches affecting 500 or more individuals "Wall of shame"
https://ocrportal.hhs.gov/ocr/breach/breach_report.jsf

HIPAA Security Rule Toolkit NIST released HIPAA Security Rule Toolkit (HSRTK) http://scap.nist.gov/hipaa/

NIST Home > Health Information Technology (IT) National Institute of Standards and Technology http://www.nist.gov/healthcare/index.cfm

American Health Information Management Association
http://www.ahima.org/

Secure Your Computer
http://onguardonline.gov/

NCHICA - North Carolina Healthcare Information and Communications Alliance, Inc.

http://www.nchica.org/HIPAAResources/Regulations.htm

Workgroup for Electronic Data Interchange (WEDI)

http://www.wedi.org

SANS - Computer Security News/Newsletters
http://www.sans.org/newsletters/

Critical Security Controls for Effective Cyber Defense
http://www.sans.org/critical-security-controls/

References

References:

1. U.S. Department of Health & Human Services
http://www.hhs.gov/ocr/privacy/
2. HIPAA Privacy, Security, and Breach Notification Audit Program
http://www.hhs.gov/hipaa/for-professionals/compliance-enforcement/audit/index.html
3. Examining Oversight of the Privacy & Security of Health Data Collected by Entities Not Regulated by HIPAA
https://www.healthit.gov/sites/default/files/non-covered_entities_report_june_17_2016.pdf
4. Guidance on Risk Analysis Requirements under the HIPAA Security Rule, The Office for Civil Rights (OCR)
http://www.hhs.gov/hipaa/for-professionals/security/guidance/index.html
5. Department of Health and Human Services, Centers for Medicare and Medicaid Services, HIPAA Security Series, 1 - Security 101 for Covered Entities, 2007.
6. Department of Health and Human Services, Centers for Medicare and Medicaid Services, HIPAA Security Series, 2 – Security Standards: Administrative Safeguards, 2007.
7. Department of Health and Human Services, Centers for Medicare and Medicaid Services, HIPAA Security Series, 3 – Security Standards: Physical Standards, 2007.
8. Department of Health and Human Services, Centers for Medicare and Medicaid Services, HIPAA Security Series, 4 – Security Standards: Technical Standards, 2007.
9. Department of Health and Human Services, Centers for Medicare and Medicaid Services, HIPAA Security Series, 5 – Security Standards: Organizational Policies and Procedures and Documentation Requirements, 2007.
10. Department of Health and Human Services, Centers for Medicare and Medicaid Services, HIPAA Security Series, 6 - Security Standards: Basics of Risk Analysis and Risk Management, 2007.
11. Department of Health and Human Services, Centers for Medicare and Medicaid Services, HIPAA Security Series, 7 - Security Standards: Implementation for the Small Provider, 2007.
12. Alberts, Christopher; Dorofee, Audrey; Stevens, James; and Woody, Carol. Introduction to the OCTAVE-S Implementation Guide, Version 1.0. Pittsburgh, PA: Software Engineering

Institute, Carnegie Mellon University, 2005. http://www.cert.org/octave
13. Nichols C., Davis N.A., Lemery C.K., Smith C.P., Medical Identity Theft. Chicago, Illinois, AHIMA 2008
14. AHIMA. "Disaster Planning for Health Information (Updated)." (Updated December 2010). Chicago, Illinois, AHIMA 2010
15. AHIMA. "HIPAA Privacy and Security Training (Updated)." (Updated November 2010). Chicago, Illinois, AHIMA 2010
16. AHIMA. "Performing a Breach Risk Assessment." Journal of AHIMA 84, no 9 (September 2013): 66-70
17. AHIMA. "Sanction guidelines for Privacy and Security Data Breaches." Journal of AHIMA 80, no 5 (May 2009): 57-62
18. Dougherty, Michelle; Washington, Lydia. "Defining and Disclosing the Designated Record Set and the Legal Health Record." Journal of AHIMA 79, no.4 (April 2008): 65-68.
19. Harris Shon, CISSP Certified Information Systems Security Professional, All-in-One Exam Guide, Fifth Edition, McGraw-Hill 2010.
20. Peter H. Gregory, CISA Certified Information Systems Auditor, All-in-One Exam Guide, Second Edition, McGraw-Hill 2012.
21. The Cost of a Data Breach, Inside Look at Ponemon Institute's 7th Annual Breach Study, Tom Field, March 23, 2012, http:// www.bankinfosecurity.com/
22. The Cost of a Lost Laptop, L. Ponemon, April 22, 2009; http://www.ponemon.org
23. Breach Resolution: 8 Lessons Learned, CEO Offers Insights Based on Experience, Howard Anderson, January 19, 2012, http://www.healthcareinfosecurity.com/
24. First-Hand Experience with a Patient Data Security Breach 12/3/11, By Micky Tripathi, President and CEO Massachusetts eHealth Collaborative, http://www.histalkpractice.com/2011/12/03/

About the author

Robert Brzezinski, MBA, CHPS, CISA spent decade leading teams through organizational changes, solving problems, improving processes, creating strategy and savings in corporate structure. Experience with small and large organizations allow Robert to find balance between SMB operational reality, small business IT and budget priorities, and regulatory requirements.

Robert continues to expand information security expertise, including cloud solutions security like Office 365 and Azure, and promotes Focus on Security and "making sense of compliance" approach, through proactive breach prevention, emphasis on staff training and integrated secure technology. He uses NIST cybersecurity framework and Center for Internet Security 20 Critical Security Controls as guidance and communication tools, to help organizations find affordable and secure solutions, that simplify SMBs IT and business. Additional information about BizWit LLC Information Security Risk Management can be found at **www.bizwit.us**

44831730R00096

Made in the USA
San Bernardino, CA
24 January 2017